K9Kitchen

Your Dogs' Diet:
The Truth
Behind
The Hype

Monica Segal AHCW

Website: www.doggiediets.com

Cover Design: Anna Borenstein
Cover Photo Image: Wernher Krutein
Editor: Marva Marrow

First Edition 2002, Toronto, Canada
Published by Doggie Diner Inc.

National Library of Canada Cataloguing in Publication
Segal, Monica
 K9kitchen : your dogs' diet : the truth behind the hype /
Monica Segal. -- 1st ed.
Includes bibliographical references and index.
ISBN 0-9730948-0-X
1. Dogs--Food. 2. Dogs--Nutrition. I. Title. II. Title: K9
kitchen.

SF427.4.S44 2002   636.7'085
        C2002-902189-8

This book is dedicated to:
Zoey who changed my life
and Cassie who teaches strength and joy.

Dr. Michael Cormier
For teaching, encouraging and showing me that
It's good to have an open mind -
But not so open that the brain falls out.

Dr. Sharon Kopinak
For challenging me to learn and "listen to the dog".

So many incredible people have put up with the crazy hours and workload that was involved in writing this book, that it's impossible to list all of them by name. I'm grateful to all, but in particular to:

My husband Morley Fruchtman - soul mate, best friend and partner in life. Thank you for believing, while being my strongest critic and staunchest supporter. Nothing would be possible without you.
Sami and Tina Segal, always urging me to follow my dreams. You're wonderful parents, incredible friends and inspirational people.
David Joseph, my ever-supportive brother. I doubt that I'd be here without you.
Stephanie Hart, sister and supportive friend. None of this would have been possible without you.
Anna Borenstein, my friend and partner in the never-ending quest for information. I'm so lucky to know you.
Mitch Wilder, helpful in so many ways, and dad to my 3rd dog – Buddy.
Laura Ottinger, always supportive and resourceful - even at midnight.
Susan Wynn DVM, continuously encouraging, supportive, resourceful and thought provoking.
Ana Hill DVM, gracious, caring and a wealth of knowledge.
Linda and Glen McKinnon, breeders who trusted that we would do whatever it took.
Marva Marrow - deadlines could not have been met without your help and enthusiasm.

All the wonderful animals that have shown and taught me about their individual needs - you have been my greatest teachers.

CONTENTS

AAFCO Guidelines For Dogs
NRC Requirements for Adult Dogs

Chapter 1
INTRODUCTION

On a quiet weekend when my dog, Zoey, was about 12 weeks old, she screamed out with pain. I'm not sure how to describe that screaming sound but if you can imagine the cry you'd have made if someone had stabbed you with a knife, you'd probably be close. My husband and I were in a panic. This had come out of nowhere. A few minutes later, Zoey screamed again and so it went every few minutes as we hurried to the car and drove to the emergency clinic. Why do these things seem to happen on weekends?

The vet took x-rays, which looked normal, and we were sent home. Zoey continued to shriek on and off until she finally had a bowel movement and things seemed to be fine after that. For a while, anyway. Her stool had never been normal from the day we brought her home but our veterinarian thought it was the dog food we were feeding her. So we switched foods over and over. Regardless of what we tried to feed this dog, her stool was full of mucus, her appetite was poor and she was lethargic.

By the time Zoey was six months old, she looked like a walking skeleton. If I'd seen a puppy in this condition, I'd have thought the owners were starving the animal. The worst part about all this was that she was actually *losing* weight by now! Desperate to find an answer, we contacted a holistic vet. This was something new for us. Both my husband and I come from a traditional background where medication was avoided if possible, but 'alternative' therapies seemed to be for kooks. Nevertheless, we felt we had nothing to lose. The vet we went to changed our lives. More importantly, she helped to save our Zoey!

After several fecal exams, Giardia was finally discovered. We really didn't know how long Zoey had harbored this pest but it seemed reasonable that it was probably for quite some time. With a dose of medication, the Giardia was eliminated but Zoey wasn't feeling much better. What to do?

According to the holistic vet, we needed to start preparing food for our dog. This was definitely a new concept! The idea seemed fine but how did one prepare food for a dog? The vet gave us a few details and suggested that I begin to do some reading. By the time I'd finished Dr. Pitcairn's book, *Natural Health for Dogs & Cats*, I was hooked. The concept made sense but now I had a million questions. Within a year I'd managed to collect and read over a dozen books on canine nutrition. Just one problem - the more I read, the more confused I became. No two authors seemed to agree on anything.

In the meantime, Zoey had been scoped and diagnosed with a severe case of colitis. She had food allergies galore. No matter which author I followed, Zoey seemed to disagree with their diets. She was now thirty percent under her optimum weight and things didn't look very promising. I decided to go back to school and get some formal training on animal and human nutrition.

This book is not meant to be a personal diary so I won't continue the story but the outcome is something that should be noted. Zoey is six years old, looking good and feeling pretty spunky! What we learned along the way is critical. We managed to arrive at a better place because we separated facts from theories. Zoey led the way and I simply followed. This book is intended to help you do the same for your beloved pet.

You will find that I am a believer in home-prepared diets, however I absolutely don't believe that there is one perfect diet program out there, and I'm about to explain why.

Chapter 2
THE DIET MAZE

Some dogs seem to do very well on a diet of processed foods. They may have a shiny coat, nice teeth, loads of energy and no obvious health problems. Mind you, it depends on what you decide a health problem is to begin with. We seem to have accepted certain things like doggie breath or a strange odor from the skin as a normal part of sharing our lives with canine friends. It doesn't have to be this way though. It certainly doesn't have to mean that cortisone injections or creams are the norm for hot spots that seem to come and go, for no apparent reason. Or that the eyes run continuously. Or that food allergies 'just happen'. I could go on and on but I'm sure you get the idea. If you live with a dog that isn't well, you *really* get the idea! Some issues are genetic and there's not much you can do about them. A lot of other problems however, can be controlled through diet. The question is what kind of diet will you choose?

There are so many processed foods on the market these days, that you could probably spend a week just reading labels and comparing ingredients. Not that many people will be able to tell what's actually in these foods because the labels remain meaningless to most. Then there are specific diets that your veterinarian probably carries. These are usually aimed at attempting to control or correct a health problem, although some are sold as a maintenance diet.

There are several books providing a variety of diet ideas for dogs. One tells you to feed a cooked diet while another explains that this is not the way to go and persuades you to feed a raw diet. One explains the benefits of feeding raw bones while another warns you of the danger of doing just this. I ought to know because I've read just about all the books out there. And for the most part, I find them confusing. How can so many authorities present so many 'facts' when the facts seem to be in opposition to each other? How can some things that are presented as facts not have any kind of printed research that we can verify? Without some kind of backup, it's an *opinion* isn't it? But I suppose that we're all entitled to have at least one of those. And if you try one of these diets and it doesn't seem to be as magical as promised, where do you turn? In particular, what do you do when the new diet worked well for a while and suddenly seemed to stop working?

Be it a processed food, a home cooked diet or a raw one, any diet may seem like a miracle cure until it starts to fail. Eventually, most diets become band-aids for a bigger problem than they can mask unless we understand some basic principles. My clients helped me to see the confusion and frustration that exists out there. There are enough books on the market to confuse most people and if that's not enough, there are internet discussion groups with as many opinions as there are members. I run one of those groups myself.

In my experience, we sometimes can't see the forest for the trees. That is to say, that some folks enjoy being right to such an extent, that they end up dismissing the dog who's desperately trying to tell them something. We read a book or three and become persuaded that a certain method of feeding makes the most sense. We choose to stand behind the author's ideas and adopt those ideas as our own. And we don't back down. Not even when our dog is in obvious distress. Books and Internet discussion groups, empower us. We can sometimes *feel* more informed than we really are. In my opinion, it should be about the dog. If it's not about that, it's simply a belief system that's like any other belief system. We're running on faith alone. That's not wise when you're trying to make decisions for an animal that has no choice but to eat what you give him or her.

My goal is to present you with facts as well as my own opinions based on my experience of working with a multitude of dogs. It would be nice if you considered my opinion but my fervent hope is that you'll gain some information that you can use from the *facts* presented.

There are a few things you should know about me. I feed a home-prepared diet to my own dogs. It's a combination of raw and cooked foods. Because of this and the success stories that I've been witness to through my clients, I don't tend to mince my words. While I won't try to persuade you to feed a certain way, I will certainly tell you the good, the bad and the ugly about different methods of feeding.

You should also know that I'm sometimes accused of complicating things. I can only say that making things too simplistic is an insult to the intelligence of the average reader and that when the full picture isn't on display, people can be led into a false sense of security. Simplicity may very well sell books but it doesn't help the person who needs answers.

Some people say that if you know how to feed your family, you also know how to feed your dog. I beg to differ. For starters, we don't know how to feed our families! If we knew half as much as we think we do, we'd be able to live much longer than we currently do. All our cells would continue to thrive because of the incredible nutrients we provided.

Our dogs don't live nearly as long as we do so the age factor comes into play. While the signs of improper diet may not affect us in any visible way for years, our dogs don't have that long. Should you ever find yourself in a position where your dog's diet isn't working and you need advice, I hope this book will be able to provide you with some clues that allow you to help your best friend(s).

Having said that, let's take a look at processed foods.

Navigating The Commercial Diets

Those glossy ads and TV commercials certainly look impressive! A gorgeous dog that appears to be vibrantly healthy and runs like the wind. Isn't that what you want for your dog? Yes, of course it is and that ad really hits home. How about the one that shows the canine senior citizen? Kind of reminds you of your own buddy doesn't it? Tired looking and maybe overweight. Oh but wait! Look what happens when that dog eats a 'complete and balanced' diet that's made for a particular age group! Amazing, isn't it? Surely you'll want some of *that* food for your aging dog. And then there's the 'complete and balanced' diet for your precious puppy. Can't forget about the importance of added calcium for the building of strong teeth and bones. Are you convinced yet? I'd suggest that most people are, which is why the processed food industry can afford to market itself so well and aim right for your heartstrings. So let's back up a minute and look at this from another angle.

The idea of total nutrition in one bowl appeals to our sense of convenience. Life becomes very simple. Rip open that bag or open that can and presto! There's nothing more to think about. But if that's true and we have the technology to create such a wonder food, why don't we eat this way ourselves? Surely it would make life easier. We could have a food labeled 'children' and another labeled 'adults' and a third for 'seniors'. Does that sound silly to you? It should. With all the wonderful, fresh foods available to us, it seems almost insane to think that we could thrive and enjoy our meals if we ate nothing but processed foods. However, even if we remove this emotional argument from the picture, the idea still doesn't make a lot of sense.

Consider the 'complete and balanced' claim. Other than the fact that this may be what the label tells us, do we really know that any food can be completely balanced and provide optimum nutrition? The truth is that we don't. Here's the real deal on dry and canned commercial pet foods.

It begins with a set standard that was arrived at by the National Research Council (NRC) and dates back to the 1980s. Then the American Association of Feed Control (AAFCO) made their own standards. AAFCO is a regulatory body that has government officials from each state who monitor animal feeds sold in their state. The pet food companies have liaisons that go to the AAFCO meetings and try to work with the AAFCO on the regulations. Having said that, we can at least say that there are *some* standards. One of the problems, however, is that many of these are *minimum* standards. So a pet food that meets minimum standards isn't quite as glorious as some ads would have us believe.

But there's more that you should know. Vitamins and minerals interact and compete with one another. Minerals do this more so than vitamins. Although the addition of vitamins and minerals to a processed food may lead us into a false sense of security about this being optimal nutrition, it isn't always the case. When a feed is formulated, many things need to be considered and the interactions between minerals are high on the priority list. So what does this mean? Well, formulations are made to consider the possibility of these interactions. For instance, copper and zinc compete. So a food that's high in copper may end up causing lower uptake of zinc and visa-versa. In order to 'balance' a food, calculations are made and an addition of zinc might be included in this instance. Does it actually balance anything? Your guess is as good as mine. There's no question that we can calculate the dietary nutrients but this doesn't really tell us much. Absorption of nutrients is the bottom line.

Absorption of Nutrients

Absorption can be tricky. Like their owners, animals are unique and may not be able to absorb the nutrients provided for any number of reasons. The source of these nutrients is crucial. Zinc oxide, for example, isn't absorbed very well so seeing this on an ingredient label doesn't actually ensure that enough zinc is available to your pet. Remember that if the diet is low in zinc, copper uptake is elevated. Copper is stored in the body and can become toxic.

The same kind of story applies to so many additions in pet foods that it becomes a mind-boggling mystery for most people to really know what's in a food. And the laws that govern labeling don't help matters.

If this isn't confusing enough, there's another piece of information you should have. Minimum nutritional requirements are standardized by looking at a population of animals and arriving at what the average animal needs. By definition, the *average* means that most of the population falls either below or above this number. Just how 'complete and balanced' can any food really be when we consider the above?

Dr. Quinton Rogers DVM PhD of UC Davis in California is a highly respected authority on canine nutrition. Dr. Rogers says "There is very little information on the bioavailability of nutrients for companion animals in many of the common dietary ingredients used in pet foods. These ingredients are generally by-products of the meat, poultry and fishing industries, with the potential for a wide variation in nutrient composition. Claims of nutritional adequacy of pet foods based on the current Association of American Feed Control Officials (AAFCO) nutrient allowances ('profiles') do not give assurances of nutritional adequacy and will not until ingredients are analyzed and bioavailability values are incorporated." (J.G. Morris, Q. Rogers)[1]

Labels

Next to advertising campaigns, the label is a key point of sale for the consumer. As we read through the various ingredients and attempt to compare them, we tend to fall for the hype. The problem is that we often don't recognize hype when we see it. Let's look at protein. There's protein in grains as well as in meat. Your dog simply isn't well adapted to eat a great deal of grain. True enough, he can survive on this kind of food but if you're aiming to provide nutrients that are easily digested and absorbed, grains aren't going to do it.

Yet grains can be the majority of the diet in processed foods. Why? They are an inexpensive source of nutrients and formulation of diets, are based on the nutrient requirements of dogs as established by AAFCO.

When a diet is put together, amino acids, are one of the considerations. If one source of food happens to be lower in an amino acid, this same amino acid can be provided through another source. That source is very often a grain. According to label laws, there has to be more of the first ingredient on a label than any of the other ingredients. When we see 'chicken' as the first ingredient, we want to believe that the majority of the food is in fact, chicken meat. But is it? Not likely. There's simply more chicken in that food than anything else. But what if there are three grains included in this can

---

[1] Q. Rogers, UC Davis, personal conversation

or bag? Obviously, there is more chicken than any *one* of the grains and so the manufacturer can legally place chicken first.

That still doesn't sound so bad, right? But ask yourself what kind of chicken is in the food. The breast or thigh? Not likely! Those are prime cuts that bring in a good dollar at the supermarket and your dog isn't likely to be eating any of that stuff.

Sometimes we see the list of grains and think it sounds nutritious. After all, what's so bad about rice, barley and oats for instance? There's nothing wrong with these ingredients but keep in mind that the protein amount you're seeing on the label includes protein from these grain sources as well. And remember that your dog is not designed to eat a diet that's heavy in grains. Your dog is not an herbivore. But even if consuming a high amount of grain was optimal (and it's not), don't think that your dog is eating the same grains you are. If food can be sold for a higher price, it is. So humans eat the good stuff and dogs get the husks, shells and floor sweepings. Don't believe me? It gets worse!

Ann Martin is the author of *Food Pets Die For* and if you haven't already read this book, I suggest that you do. Ms. Martin says "Dogs and cats euthanized at clinics, pounds and shelters are sold to rendering plants, rendered with other material and sold to the pet food industry." This statement might seem sensational and many people I spoke to when this book was first published, adamantly denied that this could be happening. After all, as pet owners, the idea that our dog could be eating our very own former pet is something that makes us cringe at best. A while ago, Toronto newspapers ran stories that proved this was indeed happening.[2] The rendering

---

[2] Toronto Star – June 5, 2001, Toronto Sun –June 4, 2001, Globe and Mail June 4, 2001

plant(s) have been using pets in the soupy mix headed for some pet foods and admitted as much. In the last few months, some of my friends in the U.S. called me to say that they had just seen the same types of reports on their television news channels.

We can look at this in two ways. The first is our natural and emotional response. Fido eating Fluffy is an outrage at this level. We can also refuse to become emotional about the news and accept that animals do indeed eat other animal carcasses if left to their own devices. However, these carcasses are fresh meat. They certainly have not been rendered and perhaps more importantly, they do not have drugs in them that were used for euthanasia.

Labels can be confusing in other ways. A common sight is the label that claims 'more' as in, 'more lamb per serving'. That appeals to us because we instinctively know that dogs crave meat and we want to provide the best food possible. But look at this claim more carefully. More lamb than *what*? A previous formula from the same manufacturer? More than the competition uses? We're bombarded with claims like 'the best nutrition', 'more' and 'higher levels', to name just three. But again, best nutrition compared to *what*? More *what*? Vitamins? Meats? Grains? Higher levels of *what*? Are higher levels a good thing? Can it be a problem if the level of this unknown ingredient is too high?

The bottom line on ads and labels is this - your dog doesn't read. These campaigns are targeted toward human appeal. 'Beef Stew' may sound tasty to you but believe me when I say that dogs prefer chunks of real meat. And if you really believe that the chunks you're seeing in a can are prime beef, you might want to re-think things. Let's be reasonable about all these claims.

Consider the price of prime ingredients. Let's suppose that a manufacturer who produces tons of food each year gets a real price break on their purchase. Now add in the cost of running that business, including the employees, ad campaigns, labels, bags, cans, distribution etc. Does it seem reasonable that a truly high quality food can cost as little as pennies per day? Price is a great motivator and manufacturers know it. But another motivator is our desire to give our dogs the same lifestyle that we seem to aim for.

Newer Label Claims

Take a look in almost any store and you're bound to notice a swing in marketing tactics. We like to think that we're more in tune with nature these days so we search for the 'all natural' claims even in our food. Antioxidants abound, supplement manufacturers are eager to get our attention, and grocery stores promote a 'fresh' produce section that includes organically grown foods. Don't think that our shift in attitude has escaped the dog food industry. There are pet foods with Glucosamine in them now. All kinds of foods have a splashy label telling us about the addition of fruits or vegetables in the bag or can. You may see flaxseed oil as an ingredient on the label but if that oil was added before the baking process, it has been rendered useless at best.

The market has changed somewhat and the pet food industry hasn't missed a beat. Some of the additions may very well be a bonus. But don't get carried away. Remember to keep your eye on the ball and look at the meat source on the label. Look at the grains in the food. Consider the source of added vitamins and minerals. Dogs don't need designer dog food.

One of the most appealing yet misleading claims that people seem to fall for is that the harder foods such as kibble will help to maintain oral health. Tarter build up requires nothing short of a chisel-like piece of equipment to remove it. I ask you to consider this while looking at a piece of kibble. How can that crunchy tidbit possibly keep teeth clean? It's not unlike claiming that pretzels can do the same thing for our own oral health. Not only is this impossible but I would suggest that as saliva combines with this food, the sticky mess actually helps to produce oral disease.

Teeth are important but gums can't be overlooked. Unless your dog has an oral 'workout', neither teeth nor gums can remain healthy. The bacteria builds up and travels through the bloodstream which can then affect more than the mouth. But don't be fooled into thinking that pearly whites translate into good dental health. Some dogs can have stained teeth and it's just that - staining. The teeth and gums may be in good condition. Other dogs have gleaming teeth but gums that are nothing short of a disaster. Either way, processed foods don't seem to help matters.

Preservatives

A discussion about processed foods wouldn't be complete without mention of preservatives. It seems obvious that preservatives are required in order to maintain shelf life. Stabilizing fats in order to prevent rancidity is a must. When we think of antioxidants, we tend to think about vitamins C and E. There are others of course, but the point is that we don't normally pop some Ethoxiquin into our mouths every morning before rushing off to work. Many commercial pet foods are preserved with chemicals such as Ethoxyquin, BHA or BHT. Some of the foods that you and I eat may contain BHA or BHT as well.

If you had a choice, would you reach for foods that contain chemical preservatives or natural ones? My personal choice would be the natural preservatives, however, pet food labels may not always tell the whole story. If the manufacturer doesn't actually *add* these chemicals when making the food, they are not obliged to state that chemicals are part of the finished product. Nevertheless, the original ingredients, which were purchased elsewhere, may indeed contain chemical preservatives.

So is it all bad news? There *is* a bit of light at the end of the tunnel. *You* have a say in this. Your dollars support the pet food industry and making yourself heard is relatively simple. While some people will choose to stay away from these foods and feed a home-prepared diet, mainstream thinking prevails and most dogs are still being fed bagged or canned diets. Looking for better quality ingredients is a step you can take right away. A defined source of meat should be on the label. In other words, 'meat' is an unknown but 'chicken' means chicken. Fewer grains in the diet, vegetables being listed on the label, natural preservatives such as vitamin E, a 'best before' date, and a manufacturer that you can reach to answer your questions, are all helpful steps. Please note that natural preservatives are a good thing but limits the shelf life of the dog food. You really don't want to buy a fifty pound bag and have it go rancid. Purchasing smaller amounts to ensure freshness is very important.

If I was feeding a processed food, I'd want to add a bit of fresh vegetables to the bowl at times. I'd also want to give my dog some plain yogurt as a treat and most certainly she'd be getting a large carrot, a chunk of lean meat or recreational bone to chew on. Before you dive in and do any of these things, please continue to read. There are benefits and risks to offering bones and other foods and you need to consider both.

Allergies

These days, so many dogs have allergies or food intolerances that just about every veterinarian I speak to considers these to be the bane of their existence. I can only imagine how the dog feels about it! Processed foods don't help matters. With so many ingredients in each food, it becomes almost impossible to point to the food culprit. Typically, this pet is switched from one processed food to another as the search for novel proteins (a protein that the dog has never eaten before) continues. Eventually, we run out of novel proteins.

Years ago, the lamb and rice diet was considered hypoallergenic. A low antigen diet (hypoallergenic is a poor term when you have intact proteins in a diet) would consist of a protein that the animal has not been exposed to. The reasoning behind this is that if the body has not yet encountered this protein, chances of a negative reaction are greatly reduced. So the lamb and rice diet seemed nothing short of miraculous since most dogs had not been exposed to lamb before.

This didn't last long, though. Since the diet seemed to be working, dogs were left to eat this diet day in and day out. The result? Many dogs developed allergic reactions to lamb. The pet food industry responded with turkey and rice followed by turkey and barley, fish and potato, duck and potato and other combinations, simply to be able to introduce novel proteins.

The end result? We now have foods on the market that have had the protein modified so that the physical characteristics of the protein molecules are changed. With a reduction of the molecular weight of the protein, the diet is now considered hypoallergenic. Most dogs, but not all, will be able to tolerate these foods, and although science has been able to come up with something that works in a sense, isn't it sad that we've had to come to this?

Does it seem logical that pets are the *only* animals on the planet that are expected to eat processed food day in and day out and thrive on it? Is it reasonable to expect that an animal can be exposed to one main protein for a lifetime and not develop a reaction? Are chemical preservatives an addition you want in your own food? Surely there's a better way, a different way, a way for dogs to do well and eat a variety of foods. That's what the rest of this book is about.

Summary

- Commercial pet foods may be 'complete and balanced' on paper but actual bioavilability of these nutrients cannot be assured.

- Mineral interactions affect the final product.

- Absorption of nutrients varies between individuals and can be hampered or increased to excess levels by mineral interactions, disease factors, genetics, etc. Pet food is formulated to meet the average requirement, which by definition, does not meet the needs of most individuals.

- The amount of protein in any diet includes proteins found in grains. High grain diets are not optimal for dogs.

- A label stating a meat source as the first ingredient may not be indicative of meat being the most abundant ingredient in the food.

- Foods preserved with chemicals offer longer shelf life. Foods that are more naturally preserved, with vitamin E, for example, should be purchased in small quantities that will be used quickly.

- Pets are the only animals on this planet that are expected to thrive on a lifetime of processed foods.

Chapter 3
THE SALES PITCH

You may already know a few people who feed home-prepared diets to their pets. While only a few years ago, this may have seemed like an odd thing to do, today more and more people give serious consideration to taking control of the ingredients they feed their dogs. After reading a book or more and discussing ideas with others, many people dive in and begin to cook meals or feed a raw diet - but it rarely happens without nerves being on edge. After all, we've been told that feeding dogs is a science and since most of us are not scientists, it's natural to be nervous.

This is especially true when your veterinarian warns you about the importance of a balanced diet. Since we are starting to understand that 'balance' may not be what we've been led to believe, we may want to question this comment. After years of believing that we are somehow incapable of feeding our pets on our own, some people take a step back and do more investigating.

Learning more will only ease your mind. The trouble is that the source of information and opposing ideas can also cause you to shake your head and give up the plan before you've begun. The flip side of this is that some people are so consumed with the zeal of converting the world to their way of feeding a dog a home-prepared diet that their sales pitch is as hard as that of any ad campaign.

The 'Don't Do It!' Warning

Your vet is a highly educated individual. She or he graduated from a respected university after years of studying. In fact, veterinarians deserve a lot of respect. Here's a doctor who must act as general practitioner, dentist, surgeon, anesthetist, and heaven knows how many other hats they wear daily. They need to know the physiology of cats, dogs, ferrets, horses and every other animal that they encounter. Our own medical doctors aren't expected to do or know nearly as much. Your veterinarian deals with the joys of a new puppy that just walked in for the first time. Twenty minutes later, he may have to put down an animal that he's known and grown emotionally attached to over the years while trying to comfort the owner. Add the 'psychiatrist' label to all the other functions vets perform.

This profession involves a great deal of knowledge, long hours and a stress load that not everyone can manage. Naturally, as in every other profession, there are people who are highly suited and skilled at their work and others who may not meet the daily demands as well. Some vets will continue to take educational courses while others won't. Some will become interested in nutrition while others will accept what they were taught and never consider other possibilities.

Given the workload that these people have and the personal interests that may vary, it's perhaps not surprising that so many vets will raise a cautious brow when someone announces that they feed a home-prepared diet. The majority of veterinarians are not given much education on canine diets. Perhaps they see no great need for it since they've been assured that everything is pretty much taken care of with prescription and maintenance diets that come from manufactures.

Much of the information that vet schools provide in this area comes directly from the manufacturers of pet foods. Still, it's presented in the typical scientific literature that seems to have been accepted by mainstream medicine. There is very little material on other ways of feeding and what there is doesn't fall into the category of scientific studies, or the studies are difficult to find and sometimes written in another language. Without studies to look at, your vet may very well feel nervous about suggesting or accepting a diet that you put together on your own.

Your veterinarian has very likely seen the results of some home-prepared diets. The dog that loves liver may have trained his owner to feed only liver, for instance. This is a disaster waiting to happen. I know of one case where the owner fed nothing but liver and cheddar cheese. The result was a very sick dog and a frustrated veterinarian. Heaven knows there are many such stories and veterinarians are well aware of them.

Thinking outside the box is one thing but *acting* outside the box can be a frightening experience for some people. Rather than doing that, it may be easier and more productive to simply add new tools to the box. One of those tools can be a home-prepared diet but without knowledge or positive experiences, it's natural for both you and your vet to have some hesitation. This may be a great time to learn together. An intelligent vet who is open minded might be quite interested in reading the same materials you are. Loan her your books or buy one as a gift for her. Work together to arrive at a place where conversation becomes easier and that toolbox becomes loaded with solid information on new ideas.

The 'You Have to Feed This Way' Command

When a pet is switched to a home-prepared diet and seems to be doing well, it's natural for the owner to be enthusiastic. Put a bunch of enthusiastic people in one room and you get a loud crowd. Add a few internet discussion groups to this and you have an overwhelming series of directives from well meaning people with what is usually limited experience. Limited, because they band together as a group that feeds one way and only to their own dogs, as opposed to a larger population of animals.

People who feed a cooked diet are convinced that this is the best way to go for a number of reasons. People feeding a raw diet are just as convinced that what they're doing is correct. In truth, it seems that many dogs do very well with a variety of feeding methods. If indeed there was one perfect answer out there, dogs would thrive only if fed one way. Since that's not the case, I'd suggest that none of us has the perfect answer for all dogs under different circumstances and with various diseases, sensitivities to foods or genetic predispositions.

The 'Commercial Diets Kill' Claim

Some people point to the commercial diets as a reason for the lifespan of dogs being so much shorter these days. They are incorrect. Most pets are, in fact, living longer lives then they were years ago. The health of these dogs during this longer period is another subject altogether and I don't personally believe that a diet of processed foods can be any more helpful to the health of our dogs than it can be to our own.

But can we truly say that commercial diets kill? This may be a stretch. One of my own dogs (that has passed on) spent sixteen years on a commercial diet. Maybe he would have lived a better life or perhaps even a longer one had I known that home-prepared diets were an option. But if I'm going to be honest, I cannot claim that the food killed him.

The 'Dogs Live Longer Due to Commercial Diets' Claim

In my opinion, this is no more a fact than claiming commercial diets kill. I would suggest that medical advances and more veterinary clinics being available have helped the lifespan. People are living longer today than we were a generation ago, despite our faster lifestyle and junk food diets. This fact doesn't translate to the diet being good. It points to medical advances and timely interventions.

The 'Commercial Diets Have Been Tested
Through Feeding Trials' Claim

True enough, some of these diets have been tested this way but not all of them. Feeding trials are an extraordinarily expensive practice and smaller manufacturers of pet foods simply can't afford to go this route. That doesn't make their foods better or worse than anyone else's. However, feeding trials may not be what you think they are. A group of dogs living in situations that do not mimic the real life of a pet are but one consideration.

The rest of the story is what makes the results sketchy at best. Your dog may be eating a particular commercial diet for the great majority of her life. This is not nearly the same thing as the dog that participates in a controlled feeding trial where the food is being fed for no more than a few weeks. Nutritional deficiencies or excesses may take years to come to light. Perhaps the most disturbing fact about feeding trials is that what's considered acceptable during the trial may not be what you or I would consider it to be. The following shows the criteria for a maintenance diet:

- All dogs that are part of the test group must be more than one year old.

- The group consists of eight dogs which must be healthy and of normal size and weight.

- Blood tests are performed at the beginning and end of the feeding trial.

- The test group must eat only the food being tested.

- By the end of the testing period, dogs must not have lost more than 15% of their original body weight.

- During the trial period, no dog must die or need to be removed from the trial due to nutritional causes of illness.

- Of the original eight dogs, six must complete the test.

- The feeding trial lasts for 26 weeks.

The Behavioral Claims

Some people think that if you feed cooked foods to a dog, you encourage begging behavior at the dinner table. Nonsense! As the leader of the pack, you give food and take it away at your choosing. A dog that begs at the table is simply hopeful that someone will give in and hand over a tidbit. If there is respect for your authority, the same dog won't beg or even come near the table when you eat. It's as simple as that. His food is in his bowl and nowhere else. That's what the dog needs to learn and any unwanted behavior has nothing to do with what you feed him.

Other people think that if you feed a dog raw meat, she will become vicious and attack other animals. Some even suggest that it's the taste of blood that makes a dog a bit crazy. Sometimes I think that we've watched too many horror movies. The dog doesn't see food in his bowl and understand that this raw meat was once a cow or chicken or what have you. It's simply food. While it's true that most dogs will gladly chase birds or other animals, this is instinct no matter what you might be feeding her.

Both begging and the need to chase are behavioral issues and neither should be confused with what the diet may be. If this was the case, we'd expect dogs that eat food that comes out of a bag to beg or become vicious when seeing bags.

In Days Gone By...

People feeding a home-prepared, cooked diet, often cite that those long-lived dogs from days gone by ate the family leftovers. People feeding raw foods claim these same dogs ate raw foods. It would seem that both feeding claims are true. In an effort to discover which of these claims might be correct, I distributed questionnaires to people who are now retired (ages 69-78) and remembered what their own parents had fed the family dogs.

Ninety-three people responded and *all* said the same thing. Most foods were cooked because the dogs ate the family leftovers. Sometimes, these dogs were thrown a raw soup bone to keep them busy for an hour and vegetable peelings were fed now and then.

For the most part however, these animals lived on foods such as pot roast, mashed potatoes, leftover soups and whatever else happened to be around or left on the dinner plates. Crusts of bread were often fed to the dogs rather than discarded and these animals were basically living on what we throw in the garbage today. Weekends were special in that the family sat down for a fancier dinner and the dogs were often treated to some first class 'people food' such as roasted meats including gravy. There was little if any thought given to calcium needs.

Most of these dogs spent some time outdoors, off leash, roaming the neighborhood. What they might have eaten there is something we can only guess at, but it seems reasonable to think that they might have supplemented their own diets with fresher foods, such as grasses, insects and perhaps a raid of a garbage can. Speculation on this point however, doesn't alter the fact that these dogs were fed at home with a diet that consisted of cooked foods for the most part, with some raw scraps thrown in.

As to the lifespan of these so called long-lived animals, the people who were good enough to put up with my multitude of questions cited that most of their dogs lived to be ten years old. One person recalled having a dog that lived to be thirteen but this was one dog amongst a group of three others in the household and seems to be the exception to the rule.

The length of a life is one issue and the health during that lifetime is another. I asked this same group of people if their dogs were generally healthy or ill. Most could not recall going to the veterinarian very often but they were quick to point out that veterinary clinics weren't as bountiful as they are today. They also commented that diagnostic and surgical procedures weren't as readily available or as advanced as they are now and that people weren't as obsessed with health as they are today.

It seems that in this city, approximately sixty to sixty five years ago, dogs were beloved family members but arthritic limps simply translated into fewer walks, dog breath was an accepted part of life and when the skin odor became too strong, the dog needed a bath. When health declined beyond what the budget could afford or the animal slowed down more than what the family thought was acceptable, the dog was put to sleep. The children were bound to find another puppy because someone down the road had a pregnant female or one that had just had pups.

In short, we may have romanticized the past in order to be able to claim that only one method of feeding is the correct way.

Summary

- Veterinarians are highly trained, busy people, who may or may not have an interest in canine nutrition. Working with your vet to arrive at some mutual understanding about diets may benefit all concerned.

- People instructing you to feed only a certain way are usually very sincere in their beliefs because they've seen good results. However, this may be true of any method of feeding when only one ideology is presented.

- There is no proof that dogs live longer or shorter lives due to being fed a certain way.

- Feeding trials performed by pet food companies do not replicate natural living conditions. The requirements for a food to pass a feeding trial may not be what some people would deem acceptable

- Do not confuse behavioral issues with food being fed.

- Claims that dogs used to eat raw or cooked foods before pet foods became popular are both correct. In Toronto, Canada, 60-65 years ago, dogs ate cooked, family leftovers, some raw vegetable peelings and the odd raw soup bone.

Chapter 4
YOUR DOG IS A WOLF

According to the latest findings, your dog is a wolf. Yes, even the tiniest Chihuahua has the wolf as an ancestor. Consider the following as presented by Dr. Susan Vargas PhD:

The genes of:
Dogs are over 85% homologous with humans
Pigs about 97%
Chimps about 99%

Dogs and wolves: 99.8 %

Depending on the source you come across, you'll find that dogs are said to have been domesticated anywhere from 10,000 years ago to 100,000 years ago or more. While this range seems great, it is beyond the scope of this book to discuss domestication and genetics in great detail. I would like to leave you with the fact, that regardless of which of these numbers is correct, it is nevertheless a very short time in the history of evolution. Most geneticists agree that breeds may look different from one another but they originated from wolves.

As such, looking at the diet of wolves is something that proponents of raw feeding may encourage. Not that most people believe we can possibly feed our pets the exact foods a wolf would have access to. The general feeling is that by looking at wolves as role models and attempting to provide foods that contain the same nutrient profiles as wild prey might have, our dogs should be able to thrive.

The adage about the whole being greater than the sum of its parts might be something to consider. Dogs may be wolves but domestication came with a price. If we look only at DNA, we have one point of view but there may be more to the story. Breeds are expected to look a certain way and in our effort to select certain traits, we may have changed things beyond what we expected. With the kind permission of Dr.Temple Grandin, I include a portion of her work below:

Overselection For Specific Traits[3]

Countless examples of serious problems caused by continuous selection for a single trait can be found in the medical literature (Steinberg *et al.*, 1994; Dykman *et al.*, 1969). People with experience in animal husbandry know that overselection for single traits can ruin animals. Good dog breeders know this. Sometimes traits that appear to be unrelated are in fact linked. Wright (1922, 1978) demonstrated this clearly by continuous selection for hair color and hair patterns in inbred strains of guinea pigs. Depressed reproduction resulted in all the strains.

Furthermore, differences in temperament, body conformation, and the size and shape of internal organs were found. Belyaev (1979) further showed that continuous selection for a calm temperament in foxes resulted in negative effects on maternal behavior and neurological problems. The fox experiments also found graded changes in many traits over several years of continuous selection for

---

[3] Genetics and the Behavior of Domestic Animals
Department of Animal Science Colorado State University Fort Collins, Colorado

tame behavior. Physiological and behavioral problems increased with each successive generation. In fact, some of the tamest foxes developed abnormal maternal behavior and cannibalized their pups. Belyaev *et al.* (1981) called this "destabilizing selection," in contrast to "stabilizing selection" found in nature (Dobzhansky 1970; Gould, 1977).

There are also countless examples in the veterinary medical literature of abnormal bone structure and other physiological defects caused by overselecting for appearance traits in dog breeds (Ott, 1996). The abnormalities range from bulldogs with breathing problems to German shepherds with hip problems. Scott and Fuller (1965) reported the negative effects of continuous selection for a certain head shape in cocker spaniels:

In our experiments we began with what were considered good breeding stocks, with a fair number of champions in their ancestry. When we bred these animals to their close relatives for even one or two generations, we uncovered serious defects in every breed. Cocker spaniels are selected for a broad forehead with prominent eyes and a pronounced "stop," or angle, between the nose and forehead. When we examined the brains of some of these animals during autopsy, we found that they showed a mild degree of hydroencephaly; that is, in selecting for skull shape, the breeders accidentally selected for a brain defect in some individuals. Besides all this, in most of our strains only about 50 percent of the females were capable of rearing normal, healthy litters, even under nearly ideal conditions of care.

Although the stress of domestication is great, Belyaev (1979) and Belyaev *et al.* (1981) concluded that selection for tameness was effective in spite of the many undesirable characteristics associated with tameness. For example, the tame foxes shed during the wrong season and developed black and white patterned fur, and changes were found in their hormone profiles. This means that the monoestrus (once a year) cycle of reproduction was disturbed and the animals would breed at any time of the year. Furthermore, changes in behavior occurred simultaneously with changes in tail position and ear shape, and the appearance of a white muzzle, forehead blaze, and white shoulder hair. The white color pattern on the head is similar to many domestic animals (Belyaev 1979). The most dog-like foxes had white spots and patterns on their heads, drooping ears, and curled tails and looked more like dogs than the foxes that avoided people.

The behavioral and morphological (appearance) changes were also correlated with corresponding changes in the levels of sex hormones. The tame foxes had higher levels of the neurotransmitter serotonin (Popova *et al.*, 1975). Serotonin is known to inhibit some kinds of aggression (Belyaev, 1979), and serotonin levels are increased in the brains of people who take Prozac (fluoxetine).

The study of behavioral genetics can help explain why selection for calm temperament was linked to physical and neurochemical changes in Belyaev's foxes. Behavior geneticists and animal scientists are interested in understanding effects on behavior due to genetic influences or those, which are due to environment and learning."

Another piece of information that might be useful comes from Early Canid Domestication.[4]

"As our breeding program has progressed, we have indeed observed changes in some of the animals' neurochemical and neurohormonal mechanisms. For example, we have measured a steady drop in the hormone-producing activity of the foxes' adrenal glands. Among several other roles in the body, the adrenal cortex comes into play when an animal has to adapt to stress. It releases hormones such as corticosteroids, which stimulate the body to extract energy from its reserves of fats and proteins."

It seems quite possible that the changes we have made through selection of breeding have affected internal workings to an extent. Perhaps one of the most important contributions to the survival of dogs is to learn to restrain ourselves from manipulating things. Be it pet food or genetics, it may be wise to appreciate that there are unwritten laws of nature. Unintended consequences may be the ultimate price that our dogs have to pay.

An animal that has compromised adrenal gland function will without a doubt have a different reaction to immune system challenges and food intolerances may be a part of that picture. While the examples above deal with foxes, breeding for specific traits is a human experiment that may show similar results with any breeding program.

At this point you may be asking yourself if the outcome of the experiments noted above would have been different had the animals

---

[4] Early Canid Domestication : The Farm Fox Experiment – Lyudmila N. Trut, American Scientist March/April 1999 Vol. 87 No.2

eaten a natural diet. The foxes did indeed eat a natural diet but I can't speak about the dogs in the first example. Either way, as a pet owner, this kind of speculation may be interesting yet pointless. Your dog is not an experiment and what you feed him or her needs to work for the individual who resides in your home *today*. Further, dogs may have differences in their ability to utilize a diet.

'Observation on food tolerance in dogs, have shown that differences occur between breeds-especially in the giant breeds which can have an increased frequency of soft stools. This may be explained at least in part by differences in the dogs' ability to utilize a diet'.

'Specific influences acting on the diet must also be addressed such as disease, the type of gut flora and the animal's susceptibility to stress as well as the affects on a particular breed. These may manifest as differences in digestive capacity, defined by the gut weight relative to bodyweight' (Meyer and others 1993).[5]

Keep in mind that the diets fed to an experimental group of Great Danes and Beagles in this case, were canned and dry food diets. Nevertheless, I've found much the same result with home-prepared diets that were not formulated to consider the individual.

The Scavenger

Without *considering* the information given above, we may wander through the diet maze in frustration. Knowing that our dogs are individuals and not simply a part of a DNA pool seems obvious. Feeding a dog for these differences however, remains a challenge. When all is said and done, dogs are scavengers. Some insist on

---

[5] Journal of Small Animal Practice 1995, Dr. J Zenteck and Dr. H. Meyer, Institut fur Tierenahrung Hannover, Germany

labeling them as carnivores while the great majority of experts deem them to be omnivores. Any way you slice it, most people would agree that dogs are as likely to raid a garbage can full of any number of things (without being very hungry) as they are to chase a bird or squirrel.

Instinct shouldn't be ignored. It can speak loudly if we're prepared to listen. Being intellectually honest would translate to looking at something while being prepared to change a previously formed opinion. In this case, the label attached to dogs seems less important than the *outcome* of our feeding method. When feeding a certain way doesn't seem to work for *your* dog, it's time to reevaluate and look at the individual rather than DNA.

Summary

- The genes of dogs are 99.8% homologous with wolves.

- DNA presents one side of the story but we may have changed internal working of dogs through the overselection for specific traits.

- Food tolerance in dogs may differ among certain breeds but may also be affected by gut flora and the affects of stress.

- Classified as carnivores by some people and omnivores by most others, dogs remain scavengers with the ability to utilize nutrients that true carnivores cannot.

- Each dog is an individual. This involves far greater consideration than what DNA classification may provide.

Chapter 5
FEEDING A RAW DIET

The idea of feeding raw meats and bones to a pet might seem frightening to some. The notion of cooked foods may seem safer but not to those who are convinced that raw foods are healthier. A line between belief systems seems to have been drawn in the sand and sometimes we seem to lose the point of the argument. If we believe in a certain method of feeding, it's usually because our own dogs are doing well with this. That doesn't for one minute translate into it being optimal for *all* dogs. I feel that I'm safe in assuming that most people want the very best for their pet(s). When they find themselves in the middle of a war zone of arguments from both sides, it can be frustrating to say the least. Let's explore the ideas behind these diets and see what might work best for *your* dog(s).

The Ideas Behind Feeding a Raw Diet

In theory, all dogs should do well on a diet that consists of raw meats, bones and some vegetables. It's only logical. As a scavenger and opportunist with great prey drive, the picture is clear. Even lacking imagination can't stop someone from picturing a dog chasing a rabbit and knowing that this is a natural event. This dog would be likely to eat the entire rabbit, so there you have your meat, bones, stomach contents if any, organs, etc. This is what usually lies behind the concept of raw diets - the notion that if we feed a diet that attempts to emulate nature, we can't go wrong.

Some people feed a whole carcass while others choose to feed parts of that carcass at different meals. For instance, I feed my dogs chicken necks or wings in the morning. The evening meal might be vegetables with liver, heart, lamb or any number of food items. It could just as easily be an egg with vegetables or whatever I feel the dogs need at the time. There isn't a very detailed plan other than the fact that I always have an assortment of foods in the freezer. And as I mentioned earlier, I also include a variety of cooked foods.

Trying to emulate Mom Nature doesn't mean that we attempt to feed a diet that a wolf might eat. That's impossible to do. Even if you can purchase venison for example, chances are that the animal wasn't caught in the bush. Farmed animals cannot possibly have the same nutrient value as their wild counterparts. They've eaten different foods and have been exposed to all the toxins in water, air and the like. So we do the best we can. Butcher shops and supermarkets become our passion as we look for a variety of foods. The truth is that wolves and wild dogs do not eat a particularly varied diet. They must survive on the prey in the region. However, people who feed raw diets are better off feeding a variety of foods. Since we already know that a 'balanced' diet is a bit of a myth, variety is an easy way to attempt to provide a full spectrum of nutrients.

Notice that I said *attempt* to provide. I'm talking about nutrients that the dog can *absorb* rather than what may be in the food itself. Our guideline for the nutrient needs of dogs comes from the NRC (National Research Council) or AAFCO. The values that have been set are based on diets of processed foods, purified diets or isolated minerals. The problem is that a home-prepared diet, be it raw or cooked, doesn't fall into any of these categories. We can spend time scratching our heads and wondering if absorption of nutrients is more or less when feeding fresh foods or we can simplify things. If indeed things were all that complicated, evolution would not have permitted us to have dogs because the species would have been extinct long ago. Knowing this, it might seem a bit silly to imagine a wild dog sitting by his den with calculator in paw as he frantically attempts to figure out what nutrients he should be striving for on his next chase of prey. Logic and observation tell us that the opportunist will eat whatever is at reach. Perhaps it would be rabbits for four days in a row followed by two days of no prey at all. Maybe next week he'll be fortunate enough to graze on some fallen berries and catch a roaming lamb.

Speculation is endless but one thing is a certainty. The wild dog or wolf is highly unlikely to be eating the same thing day in and day out. He's unlikely to be eating daily for that matter! Nutrients come naturally and in the form of variety. Nothing is a complete and balanced meal. Not for humans, nor other animals.

If you're reading this and feeling queasy at the idea of actually feeding raw meat to your pet, you're in good company. I don't know too many people who simply read something and threw raw meat at the dog the following morning. It may happen but it's not the norm. Most of us eased into this and took some deep breaths while waiting for the dog to keel over. I often joke that when I first gave Zoey raw chicken, I had one hand on the cell phone for the vet and the other on my car keys. Not surprisingly, nothing happened other than she ate her food. But there are situations when you might want to reconsider feeding this way so let's talk about it.

Imaginary and Real Risks

Cooked bones are not going to be discussed here other than to warn you that they can splinter and cause severe damage to the entire intestinal tract from the mouth to the bowel. Cooked bones are not even a consideration so please forget that they exist. We are discussing *raw* bones only.

Raw bones can cause fecal impaction. Some people do offer a bare bone now and then. Most of us however, feed raw bones *with meat* still on them. Chicken wings, chicken necks, turkey necks, etc.

Overfeed these and there is still a risk of fecal impaction. Bones tend to firm up the stool so you don't want to go overboard.

Choking on whole, meaty bones happens sometimes. Some people who feed whole bones are quick to justify their decision to feed this way. After all, the teeth are incredibly clean from the chewing the dog has to do. The gums are exercised. The jaws are exercised. Heck, the entire dog is exercised if a whole carcass is fed. But yes, choking can happen just as it can happen on dry food, sticks, and any other number of items. It is also the case when the piece of food is larger than what the esophagus can handle. Feeding a turkey neck to a Toy Poodle is not the same thing as feeding it to a German Shepherd Dog and even the Shepherd can choke on it.

Many dogs are excellent chewers and not overly greedy so they seem to do a great job of handling whole, meaty bones. Then there are dogs like my Zoey. She's a gulper and to top it all off, she's always in a big hurry to eat so she can get back to work. Add these behaviors to the fact that her colitis flares up to the point of bloody diarrhea for days on end and you might agree with me that grinding raw meaty bones makes sense.

I'm presenting these ideas so that you can begin to really watch your dog. Does he chew slowly? Does she take a bone and run off with it so that you're unable to see what's happening? These are only two of the questions you can ask yourself before deciding whether feeding whole bones is riskier than what seems reasonable or if your dog is likely to be the perfect example of a methodical chewer.

If in doubt, grind! Regardless of the claims to the contrary, I can honestly say that teeth *do* manage to remain quite clean even though the food is ground. A chunk of raw meat that needs to be chewed and scraped can be the middle ground. Raw meaty bones can be ground and chunk meat can be fed with less risk if this concerns you.

Raw bones can splinter. Some people claim that raw meaty bones will not do this but I maintain that raw bones can and do splinter at times. Nobody knows what percentage of raw fed dogs have had this occur and frankly, I'm not sure it matters. When it's *your* dog on the operating table, *your* statistic is 100%. This doesn't mean that I'm suggesting a high risk factor but rather, pointing out a possibility that may concern you. If you're worried, grind the raw meaty bones and have a good night's sleep.

Some people are worried about dogs breaking teeth when chewing on bones. Yes, it can happen but the great majority of dogs that I know have never had this problem. The large, thick bones such as marrow or soup bones tend to be the culprits whereas the softer bones, from chicken for example, are not as likely to be the cause of broken teeth. It also depends on your breed and your use of common sense. Feeding large beef bones to a small dog is more likely to end up being problematic than the same bones would be for a large dog. Consider the shape of the mouth, the strength of the jaw, and make your decision.

Bacteria

Let me preface the following by saying that bacteria exists in all kinds of foods including pet foods in cans and bags. It can exist in cooked foods as well, so the information presented is not intended to sway you towards a certain way of feeding. Of all the questions I'm asked, the one about salmonella is the most common.

Salmonella is high on the list when we think of bacteria in raw meat. E. Coli is another. There are many, many more. Some people claim that dogs are immune from the bacteria in raw meats but the truth is that dogs can and do become sick from them sometimes. Certainly the majority of dogs seem to do just fine, and do not become clinically diseased, but then there are the other ones.

There is a problem in diagnosing these things at times. The most common symptom of salmonellosis (salmonella poisoning) is enteritis (inflammation of the intestinal tract). There are different strains of salmonella and they differ in their ability to cause disease. This correlates with their ability to invade the mucosa of the intestine. The problem in diagnosing salmonellosis is that despite a negative culture result, the organism may still be at work in the body. Salmonella is notoriously difficult to culture and especially so when other bacteria are present in the sample. As fecal samples are full of various bacteria anyway, you can see the dilemma. Some people don't concern themselves with bacterial diseases and claim that even vets can't point to any studies that show a problem with salmonella in particular. Now you know why. It's simply not an easy thing to find.

The immune system is complex and under normal conditions, the intestinal tract is protected from disease causing organisms. The normal motility of the intestines propels ingested infectious organisms like salmonella to the large intestine where a healthy resident bacteria resides. Under normal circumstances, this resident bacteria prevents the salmonella organisms from colonizing and multiplying within the gut. Mucus secreted by the mucosal lining of the intestine contains cell mediated immune factors that protect the gut from disease causing organisms. It is for all these reasons that it is not uncommon to culture salmonella from clinically healthy animals.

Keep in mind that 'clinically' healthy means that the animal is not displaying any symptoms. When we see a bright and happy dog with a lot of energy, shiny coat and pearly white teeth, it's understandable to think that the animal is indeed the picture of health. But is that really so?

Welcome to the world of subclinical carriers. When the body is attacked by an organism, there are three possible outcomes. In the best case scenario, we may never even know that the body fought a battle. It simply wins the war and all is well. On the opposite side of the fence, the immune system loses and disease takes hold with a variety of possible outcomes. And then there is the middle ground. The immune system launches an attack and is able to stop the manifestation of disease but the animal becomes a subclinical carrier. In other words, this animal quietly carries an organism that he or she will shed in feces, nasal discharges and so on. If this same animal is suddenly under stress and becomes ill for another reason, it is possible that the organism he was carrying begins to surface.

This long-winded explanation is simply to show you that what you see isn't always what you get in the long run. While a pet that sheds an organism may pose a threat to the owner with a compromised immune system and to other pets (poop sniffing helps to spread disease), it is the breeder who is likely to notice a problem first.

All dogs may seem healthy until perhaps there is a pregnancy. The added stress of whelping can turn the subclinical carrier into a problem. She may give birth to a weak litter or a litter that dies soon after birth. The search for the diet culprit may begin but in my experience, many breeders look at the nutrients rather than considering the possibility of disease.

An example would be a client of mine who bred her lovely girl only to wait for the whelping of four puppies that died shortly after birth. This was the second time that an otherwise healthy female couldn't seem to whelp a normal litter and produced a rather defiant case of diarrhea afterwards. After several discussions and a few tests, it was discovered that the pups and mom had salmonellosis.

Well good grief, if this is the sort of scary stuff that can happen, why on earth would anyone feed a raw diet? That's a valid question however, there's more to the story so don't panic quite yet.

Disease Factors

Ever wonder why your cousin always seems to get a cold when you don't? Why your brother seems to have chronic gastric upsets and nobody else in your family suffers from this? The immune system has a lot to do with it and many things can affect the immune system status to begin with.

Nutritional status shouldn't be overlooked. Studies in dogs have shown that overfeeding and obesity tend to decrease the resistance to salmonellosis although the reason for this is uncertain. Dietary deficiencies of choline and methionine in pregnant dogs will increase susceptibility of their offspring to salmonellosis. Keep in mind that choline is found in egg yolks, lecithin, meat and whole grain cereals, all of which may be a part of a home-prepared diet. Methionine is an essential amino acid supplied in good amounts by eggs, fish, garlic and meat, to name just a few foods that can be a part of a home-prepared diet.

Age is also a factor. Young animals tend to be more susceptible to infection and clinical disease than are the adults. The kids acquire some immunity from mom's colostrum and milk but there's a bit of a problem. During the time that this immunity is viable, pups are not able to acquire immunity from being exposed to a certain antigen. So until the pup is a few weeks old, he is reliant on mom's antibodies to help him out. This leaves a window of opportunity for infection to set in. Older animals, which have not yet been exposed to the salmonella antigen through a natural challenge are also at greater risk. In utero infection results in either death and absorption of fetuses, or in the birth of weak and sickly pups that usually die.

Finally, immunodeficiency should be a consideration. Malnutrition, concurrent diseases and prolonged treatment with steroid drugs are some of the conditions that suppress the dog's immune system. An ill animal will be more predisposed to infectious disease such as salmonellosis than a healthy animal. This doesn't mean they *will* become ill but the risk is greater.

The information above is meant to discuss the reasons you may opt for a cooked diet rather a raw one. If you pet is ill at the moment, feeding a cooked diet might make sense. If *you* have a very weak immune system, you might choose to feed a cooked diet or be very careful when feeding a raw one. A healthy dog is capable of becoming ill from the salmonella bacteria but this is not the norm.

There Are Positives to Raw Feeding

Healthy animals seem to do great battle with various organisms and win the day. I can't say that there is no risk involved when feeding a raw diet but in my opinion, there is risk in any type of feeding. It's a matter of weighing the pros and cons. Raw foods contain unaltered enzymes and amino acids. Raw fat is usually more easily digested than cooked fat. The unaltered nutrient profile in raw foods means that we may be offering nutrients we haven't yet discovered. Raw foods offer a full spectrum of natural vitamins and minerals. The disease fighting nutrients in raw foods are being discovered almost daily. Oral health seems to be maintained whether or not you choose to feed whole meaty bones or grind them.

As for the fear of bacteria, understand that your dog may very well be eating insects when in the yard and insects carry bacteria too. Dogs may eat dirt and heaven knows what might be living in *there*. This may also be a good time to remind you that if your dog eats his own feces or that of other animals, he is already receiving a heavy duty bacterial load. Should I mention that when your dog licks his private areas, there is bacteria there as well?

Considerations

Despite the possible benefits of raw diets, there is something to keep in mind. If your dog has gastrointestinal problems, the mucosal lining of the gut may be damaged. If your dog has been taking antibiotics for an extended period of time, the immune system will not be nearly as robust as we'd like it to be. Raw foods do contain bacteria that healthy dogs seem to combat but an ill dog may not be as fortunate. I would strongly suggest that you *ease* into raw foods in these cases. Your dog may still be able to eat this way and in fact, may thrive, but I personally believe it's best to watch, learn and *then* take action. In my experience, dive-bombing a compromised immune system with a bacterial load that it may or may not be able to carry is an unnecessary risk.

Finally, please note that most of the bacterial problems I know of came about due to improper meat handling. Yes, your dog can handle some bacteria that you can't. Yes, it's easy to become lazy and feed meat that's been on the counter for the last eight hours. No, not all dogs will become ill from this practice. But when all is said and done, I'm asking you to please use some common sense.

Shopping for meats and leaving them in your car when it's sweltering outside is just silly. Thawing meat on the counter may be risky. You might do this two hundred times and not see a problem but eventually, it can catch up with you. Buying the prepackaged, ground meats that are available at grocery stores can be more risky. The butcher is not likely to stop the grinder hourly in order to thoroughly wash it in hot, soapy water. In this case, the grinder becomes more highly contaminated as the day goes on, and any meat that's being ground in it also becomes contaminated. If you prefer ground meats, buying your own grinding machine is a safer way to go. I'm saying that there seems little point in testing waters to see just how much bacteria your dog can handle. This is not an experiment. This is your dog's life so why take the risks?

Don't forget that even if your dog can handle a huge load of bacteria, chances are that you and your family cannot. Babies often take a toy from the floor and stick it in their mouths. If that floor had raw meat on it, there is potential risk of disease to the baby. Countertops, sponges and utensils should be thoroughly washed in very hot water with soap. A final rinse with vinegar or bleach rather than plain water is an added precaution if you're concerned. Wash the feeding and water bowl in hot, soapy water and do it sooner rather that later. A bowl that sits on the floor for hours on end is bound to allow bacteria to multiply.

This way of feeding doesn't always have to be dangerous unless we make it so. After all, unless we're vegetarians, we handle raw meat for own families. Feeding the same meat to your dog doesn't mean that you are excused from using common sense and practicing basic hygiene.

Winging It

There is a *real* risk to feeding a raw diet that many people don't even think about. Whether it's because chicken is easily found in supermarkets or the price is attractive, a lot of people gear the entire diet around this bird. If you intend to grind raw, meaty bones the way I do, chicken simplifies life because necks and wings go through the electric grinder easily. There's nothing wrong with using chicken as a *part* of the diet but it should not be the only protein source. Just as no other meat should be the only protein source.

Always remember that your goal is to provide nutrients and each food is limited in value. There is nothing wrong with chicken per se but it is much lower in zinc, for instance, than lamb. Say your dog can't handle another meat source. Then you have no choice but to use chicken but remember that the bird has many parts. There's more to it than just wings and necks. Use gizzards for zinc content. Use the liver for some vitamin A and folate. If your dog can eat eggs, use them. They're the perfect protein. Consider using fish at times. Try as best you can to offer more than chicken as a meat source. If that is impossible due to food allergies, seriously consider using a multi vitamin/mineral tablet made for pets. A company called Thorne Research makes one by the name of Canine Basic Nutrients that I think is good and many vets can supply it.

Reminder

Please note that this chapter includes lengthy explanations of the potential risks of a raw diet. This is simply due to the fact that attempting to cover all possibilities while explaining *how* these risks are made possible takes time and space. In contrast, the possible benefits of a raw diet are relatively straight forward. I feed my own dogs a diet that includes raw foods. It is hoped that this chapter will allow you to examine the benefits of raw foods while providing information on much debated subjects such as bacteria.

Summary

- Raw foods provide unaltered amino acids, vitamins and minerals as well as undiscovered nutrients that may play vital roles.

- Grinding raw meaty bones eliminates the fear of choking and/or pieces of bone piercing the digestive tract.

- Oral health can be maintained despite raw foods being ground.

- Excessive bone consumption can cause fecal impaction.

- Harmful bacteria reside in many places - including foods.

- Diseases caused by bacteria are dependant on the health status of the individual and the abundance and/or aggressiveness of the bacteria itself. Proper home care and hygiene can go a long way to reduce risks of infections.

- Clinically diseased animals show symptoms of disease. Subclinical carriers are animals that may display no symptoms but have the ability to infect others. Subclinical carriers may become clinically diseased themselves during times of stress or illness due to other causes.

Chapter 6
NUTRIENTS IN RAW, MEATY BONES

Meaty bones that are in a raw state are touted as being chock full of nutrients. I've read many books that promote these foods and wondered what exactly was in them. While everyone I asked had some sort of rough idea of the nutrient content, it seemed unlikely to me that a diet based on 60% chicken necks, for example, was equivalent to a diet that was based on 60% chicken backs yet, many people feed these parts interchangeably. This is especially the case for people who live with dogs that cannot handle more than one protein source.

There are so many unknowns in the world of nutrition and I'm one of those people who just can't help asking questions. When nobody could give me the information I wanted, working with a lab helped to provide some answers. It would have been interesting to look at a greater variety of raw, meaty bones than I did but there were two problems. One was that in order to do an analysis, these things had to be ground and no butcher would agree to attempt to grind items such as lamb bones. It seems that even heavy duty, professional grinding machines can break under the strain of very hard bones. The other point that I considered is that most people have access to a limited variety of raw meaty bones. For these reasons, I chose to present the items that the majority of people use as part of a raw diet. The items that are most easily found at butcher stores, natural food markets and grocery stores.

Please note that the samples were gathered from a variety of stores in order to obtain a more general picture. Had all samples come from the same location on the same day, I don't believe that the results would be indicative of the way most of us shop. You might purchase a batch of chicken wings today and another in a month. There are bound to be differences depending on what the source of these food items are, how fresh they are, etc.

The analysis of rabbit does not include the head but does include the organs. While it would have been interesting to see the results of an analysis that *did* include the head, the fact remains that most butchers and supermarkets do not offer rabbit this way and I wanted to show nutrient values for foods that were readily available to most people.

You will also notice that several samples of each food were analyzed. There are large variations in the content of individual samples and lab errors are possible. Using one or two samples would have been far less time consuming and certainly less costly, but the results would have been meaningless.

Turkey Necks (skinless) 100 gr. – as fed basis

Test	Maximum Value	Minimum Value	Mean	Sample size
Moisture	71.2	67.59	68.94	8
Protein	17.84	17.3	17.70	8
Calcium	2.59	1.54	1.84	8
Phosphorus	1.39	.78	1.0	8
Sodium	0.58	0.53	0.54	8
Potassium	0.24	.22	.23	8
Magnesium	0.06	0.04	0.05	8
Zinc (ppm)	43.87	42.22	42.72	8
Manganese (ppm)	<1.0	<1.0	<1.0	8
Copper (ppm)	<1.0	<1.0	<1.0	8
Iron (ppm)	13.24	9.21	10.90	8
Ash	10.72	5.41	7.52	8
Fat	4.25	3.43	3.75	8
Calories	119	112	116	8
Carbohydrates	3.55	0	1.10	8

Chicken Necks (skinless) 100 gr. – as fed basis

Test	Maximum Value	Minimum Value	Mean	Sample Size
Moisture	70.42	64.4	68.95	10
Protein	17.07	13.70	15.13	10
Calcium	1.47	0.89	1.15	10
Phosphorus	.98	0.5	0.70	10
Sodium	0.11	0.8	0.9	10
Potassium	0.16	0.13	0.15	10
Magnesium	0.05	0.03	0.04	10
Zinc (ppm)	30.71	24.36	28.82	10
Manganese (ppm)	<1.0	<1.0	<1.0	10
Copper (ppm)	<1.0	<1.0	<1.0	10
Iron (ppm)	24.4	17.2	19.86	10
Ash	5.04	4.10	4.63	10
Fat	10.96	8.19	9.46	10
Calories	189	148	164	10
Carbohydrates	2.32	0	0.65	10

Chicken Wings 100gr. – as fed basis

Test	Maximum Value	Minimum Value	Mean	Sample Size
Moisture	61.85	58.91	60.48	8
Protein	17.09	15.61	16.57	8
Calcium	1.15	0.67	0.92	8
Phosphorus	0.66	0.43	0.55	8
Sodium	0.08	0.06	0.07	8
Potassium	0.18	0.15	0.17	8
Magnesium	0.04	0.02	0.03	8
Zinc (ppm)	18.81	12.65	16.49	8
Manganese (ppm)	<1.0	<1.0	<1.0	8
Copper (ppm)	<1.0	<1.0	<1.0	8
Iron (ppm)	28.77	12.37	21.46	8
Ash	4.11	3.10	3.53	8
Fat	21.14	18.83	19.63	8
Calories	253	234	244	8
Carbohydrates	0	0	0	8

Chicken Backs (with skin) 100 gr. – as fed basis

Test	Maximum Value	Minimum Value	Mean	Sample Size
Moisture	65.13	56.91	60.97	8
Protein	15.64	14.91	15.31	8
Calcium	1.81	1.08	1.33	8
Phosphorus	0.97	0.62	0.74	8
Sodium	0.11	0.09	0.20	8
Potassium	0.19	0.14	0.17	8
Magnesium	0.05	0.02	0.04	8
Zinc (ppm)	26.48	21.79	23.05	8
Manganese (ppm)	<1.0	<1.0	<1.0	8
Copper (ppm)	<1.0	<1.0	<1.0	8
Iron (ppm)	46.25	19.21	33.41	8
Ash	4.41	3.04	3.68	8
Fat	22.91	15.63	17.15	8
Calories	224	202	208	8
Carbohydrates	0.87	0	0.30	8

Rabbit 100 gr. – as fed basis

Test	Maximum Value	Minimum Value	Mean	Sample Size
Moisture	74.6	69.2	72.9	10
Protein	18.44	17.28	17.79	10
Calcium	0.81	0.52	0.65	10
Phosphorus	0.69	.037	0.46	10
Sodium	0.07	0.06	0.063	10
Potassium	0.24	0.23	0.233	10
Magnesium	0.04	0.03	0.032	10
Zinc (ppm)	20.85	15.41	17.43	10
Manganese (ppm)	<1.0	<1.0	<1.0	10
Copper (ppm)	<1.0	<1.0	<1.0	10
Iron (ppm)	17.25	10.62	12.71	10
Ash	5.41	2.76	4.18	10
Fat	8.51	4.36	5.76	10
Calories	150	109	127	10
Carbohydrates	0.40	0	0.05	10

The following is presented with the permission of Dr. Jurgen Zentek. Although Dr. Zentek was unable to confirm which bones this pertains to, it may nevertheless be of interest to some readers.

Calf /Pig Bones 100 gr. - as fcd basis:

	Calf	Pig
Dry matter	79g	83g
Organic matter	45g	40g
Raw ash	34g	43g
Raw protein	23g	17g
Raw fat	21g	21g
Raw fiber	0g	0g
Energy	1.39MJ	1.26MJ
Digestible protein	10.4g	7.7g
Usable energy	0.87MJ	0.82MJ
Linoleic acid	0.4g	0.6g
Isoleucine	0.62g	
Leucine	1.23g	
Lysine	1.14g	
Methionine	0.31g	
Cystine	0.33g	
Phenylalanine	0.70g	
Histidine	0.40g	
Threonine	0.73g	
Tryptophan	0.26g	
Valine	0.84g	

Are These Numbers Meaningful?

Answering this question depends on your belief system and mind set. If you look at Mom Nature and let Her be your guide, you may not care what the nutrients in bones are to begin with. Or you may be curious, but since the diet you provide your dog is based on variety without more 'scientifically' approved notions, numbers can be shrugged at and ignored. If this works for you and your dog, great!

My own thoughts are based on my experience. I tend to work with dogs that have *not* done well on a feeding method that involves some of this and some of that without much calculation.

My clients include people who believe that numbers can have some meaning and others who never really thought about it until a problem arose. The bottom line for me is that unless I can look at a diet and put some values to the nutritional content, correcting the diet is nothing short of a guessing game. This is especially true in the case of calcium and the skeletal problems that some dogs develop. So for better or worse, I use the NRC guidelines and I can truly say that this has worked very well. I know that the guidelines were not based on real foods but this has been working for me for years. It is not in the spirit of the free and natural feeding methods that some people believe in, but I find that working within a guideline makes the difference between being able to help the dog and guesswork.

You may be asking yourself how I feed my own dogs since I mentioned earlier that they don't eat foods that are part of a particularly detailed plan. While I'm not concerned with feeding all known nutrients at one meal or in one day, my dogs *do* eat the correct foods to ensure that the nutrients are in the correct amounts. At least on paper. Absorption, as we've discussed, is an unknown variable most of the time.

An adult dog is usually able to look and perform well even though she or he is lacking in nutrients, or perhaps dealing with an excess of some nutrients. This speaks loudly about the adaptability of these animals. The problem is that *because* the dog seems to do well, we can be stumped when this same dog begins to do poorly. Diet may not even be considered at that point since history would indicate that the diet had been working for years.

Mineral Interactions

Minerals don't take a day off. Think of the body as a bank. It has a certain amount of money. You withdraw some today and replace it tomorrow. The balance remains the same in the long run. Sometimes you withdraw more often than you replace. The account starts to look a little shabby. You might have a 'sickly' account that is now fairly vulnerable should an unexpected expense come up. Think of the body stores of minerals as the bank and disease as the unexpected expense. Now imagine a bankruptcy. This is what happens when the body is left to use all of its stores.

At first, despite the diet being less than optimal, you may not notice any changes in your dog. He might even look *better* than in the past. How can this be?

Remember that your adult dog has a reserve of nutrients in the storage houses of the body, such as the bones and liver to mention only two. The body calls upon these reserves to compensate for any lacking nutrient. While these reserves are being used and slowly depleted, the diet may indeed have optimal nutritional value of other nutrients. An example of this would be a diet that lacks in calcium but offers excellent zinc content. Since zinc is important for healthy skin (among other things), a dog that suffered from flaky skin may suddenly be looking wonderful. However, the calcium stores are slowly being depleted.

The chart on mineral interactions (fig 1.1) shows the incredible work that the body does without our ever thinking about it. This 'dance' between minerals translates into competition so that absorption of one mineral may be dependent on the presence or absence of another.

This chart is not something you need to memorize or fret over, but I hope that it can help you if or when your dog isn't doing well on any given diet. It should also help you to understand the need for a variety of foods when preparing meals for your dog. By looking at the basics of mineral interactions, you can see that by repeating the same meals with the same nutrient profiles, you risk repeating the same mineral interactions as well. Since so many minerals compete with each other, we want to keep this competition varied in order to provide nutrients the body can *absorb*. This is what lies behind my insistence that you feed a variety of foods rather than base all meals on chicken, which so many people seem to be doing. It is also why you really need to think about providing a multi vitamin/mineral tablet if your dog can eat only one type of protein.

The Minerals in Raw, Meaty Bones

Due to mineral interactions, a question arises about the analyses presented. While it is interesting to see what minerals these raw, meaty bones contain, I still don't know how much of any nutrient is actually being absorbed. The calcium to phosphorus ratio in these samples is wonderful and to be expected. However, calcium binds zinc and leaves less zinc available to the body. Is the zinc content of raw meaty bones actually available to our pets? What about the other minerals? Until there is a controlled feeding trial, we can't really know these things in a way that scientists would accept.

Still, there are some basic guidelines which I follow and I've yet to see these fail me. Some veterinary nutritionists use the NRC nutrient guidelines and multiply the values by 1.25 - 1.5. The reasoning behind this is simple. The nutrient guidelines don't necessarily allow for mineral competition. The guidelines are also based on the 'average' and as we've already discussed, this allows most dogs to fall either below or above the average in a group. Thirdly, just because Mother Nature included X amount of minerals in a food doesn't mean that She intended for all the minerals to be absorbed at a rate of one hundred percent.

In my experience, calculations have their place and when a diet isn't working or has stopped working well for the dog, it's time to look at nutrient values. I use the NRC guidelines sometimes without increasing them because I haven't found much need to do it. The odd time that I've tried using the 1.5 method, results were poor. Perhaps the nutrients in real foods are not needed in as great amounts as what some may suggest are needed in a highly processed diet. I wish I could say this with certainty but my only evidence is anecdotal. I *do* increase the suggested NRC nutrient values when a dog has been deficient in a nutrient for quite some time. In those cases, I increase nutrient content for a few months or until improvement is evident. Depending on the situation, I may opt to remain with these higher values.

The AAFCO guidelines provide higher nutrient values and contain more listings of vitamins and minerals. You can see both the AAFCO and NRC guidelines on pages 67 and 68.

With any luck, you will never need to think about much of this. Your dog may do very well with a variety of foods and there would be no need to concern yourself with the feeding industry guidelines and calculations. However, should you find that your best friend isn't doing well and you need to dig for answers, it is my hope that this chapter can help to guide you.

Summary

- Minerals don't take a day off. They interact with each other constantly.

- The body has storage houses of minerals. Due to this, it is possible to feed an inferior diet yet see improvement in health. The diet may provide a good supply of a mineral that the body *had* lacked while using up the stored amount of another mineral. In time, this mineral will be lacking and new health problems can arise. Example: New diet offers good zinc content and skin improvement is noted. The same diet is lacking in calcium and calcium stores are being depleted.

- When a diet has been working well for a period of time and the dog suddenly seems to be doing poorly due to a new problem, it may be wise to consider mineral interactions and take a closer look at the nutrient values of foods.

Figure 1.1:
Mineral Interactions

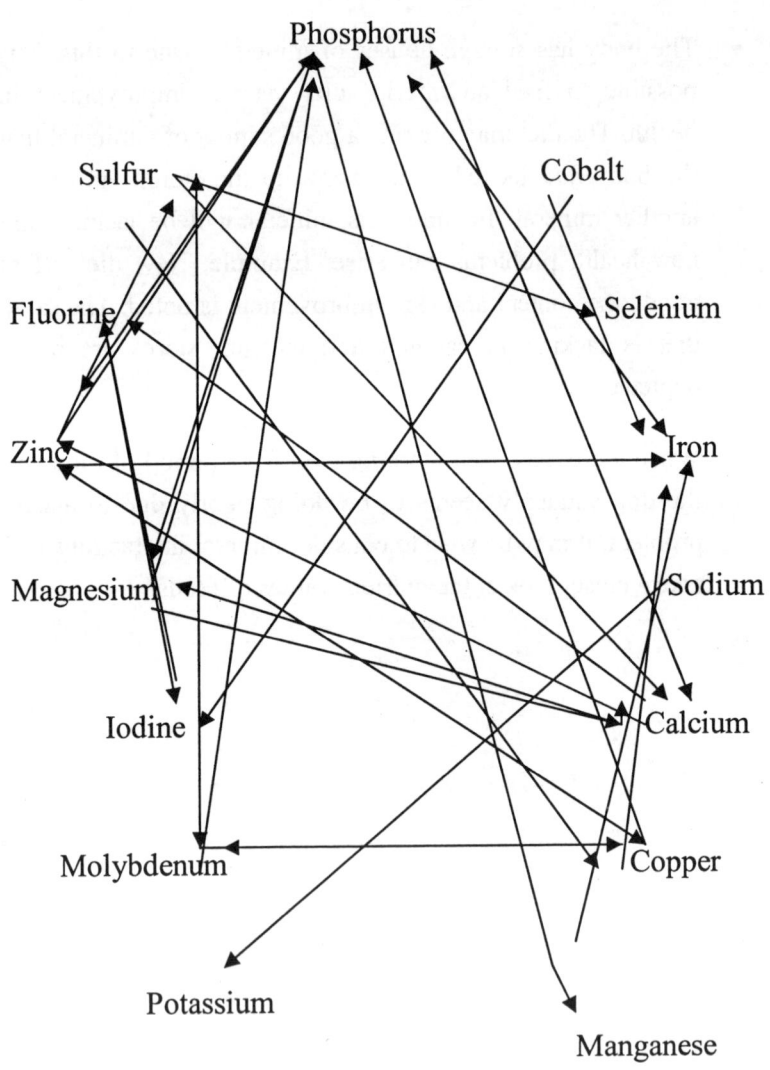

AAFO Guidelines for Adult Dogs (dry matter basis)

Protein	Minimum		18%
Fat			5%
Calcium	0.6%	Maximum	2.5%
Phosphorus	0.5%	Maximum	1.6%
Potassium	0.6%		
Sodium	0.06%		
Chloride	0.09%		
Magnesium	0.04%	Maximum	0.3%
Iron	80 mg/kg	Maximum	3,000 mg/kg
Copper	7.3 mg/kg	Maximum	250 mg/kg
Manganese	5 mg/kg		
Zinc	120 mg/kg	Maximum	1000 mg/kg
Iodine	1.5 mg/kg	Maximum	50 mg/kg
Selenium	0.11 mg/kg	Maximum	2 mg/kg
Vitamin A	5000 IU/kg	Maximum	250,000 IU/kg
Vitamin D	500 IU/kg	Maximum	5.000 IU/kg
Vitamin E	50 IU/kg	Maximum	1,000 IU/kg
Thiamine	1 mg/kg		
Riboflavin	2.2 mg/kg		
Pantothenic Acid	10 mg/kg		
Niacin	11.4 mg/kg		
Pyridoxine	1mg/kg		
Folic Acid	0.18 mg/kg		
VitaminB12	0.22 mg/kg		
Choline	1200 mg/kg		

NRC Requirements for Adult Dogs (as fed basis)
Per kg of body weight

Vitamin A	75 IU/kg
Vitamin D	8 IU/kg
Vitamin E	0.5 IU/kg
Vitamin K	2 mcg/kg (noted as not required unless antibiotics are being given for an extended period of time
Thiamin	20 mcg/kg
Riboflavin	50 mcg/kg
Pantothenate	200 mcg/kg
Niacin	225 mcg/kg
Pyridoxine	22mcg/kg
Folic Acid	4 mcg/kg
Biotin	No dietary requirement noted
Vitamin B12	0.5 mcg/kg
Choline	25 mg/kg
Calcium	119 mg/kg
Phosphorus	89 mg/kg
Sodium	11 mg/kg
Potassium	89 mg/kg
Chloride	17 mg/kg
Magnesium	8 mg/kg
Iron	0.65 mg/kg
Copper	0.06 mg/kg
Manganese	0.10 mg/kg
Zinc	0.72 mg/kg
Iodine	0.012 mg/kg
Selenium	2.2 mcg/kg

Chapter 7
COOKED FOODS

Many dogs thrive on cooked foods. After reading that dogs come from wolves and that their natural diet is obviously raw, it may seem odd if not downright silly to consider a cooked diet. Yet, I can attest to the robust health of many dogs that have lived on cooked foods for an entire lifetime. Would they have fared better on a raw diet? Perhaps. Can I guarantee that this would have been the case? No. Does anyone have statistics to prove that raw fed dogs live longer and/or healthier lives than their cousins who eat a home cooked diet? Not that I'm aware of.

The most common reason that some of my clients prefer to cook for their pet is the fear of bacteria in raw foods. Certainly, cooking seems to dispel that fear. However, other than this argument, there are situations when cooked foods may be a good option.

Gastric Upsets

Many of my clients have dogs with gastrointestinal problems of one sort or another. In these cases, cooked foods are often better tolerated than raw foods might be. Sometimes the condition is so severe that even cooked food is not tolerated well. Baby food comes to the rescue in these cases. A mild and easy to digest option, baby food such as pure chicken in broth combined with a small amount of vegetable or rice seems to help.

Pancreatitis

A diet for pancreatitis needs to be very low in fat and easily digested. While we might think that lean, raw meats would be the natural and optimal way to feed a dog with this condition, my experience shows otherwise. By lightly poaching lean meat, the small amount of fat that can be drained away, makes a huge difference in the recovery time of the dog. Unfortunately, I've had my fair share of experience with this condition and in every case, once the dog was eating *cooked*, lean meats rather than *raw*, lean meats, health returned in a much shorter period of time.

Grains

Feeding grains to dogs has become a widely discussed topic. There has not been an established requirement for grains in the canine diet, but neither has there been any proof that the nutrients in grains are not well utilized. It would seem obvious that wolves are not eating cooked oats and rice, but I don't work with the owners of wild wolves. Some of my clients live with dogs that not only do well with some grain in the diet but they seem to need it. While others may have experienced different results, I find that Golden Retrievers, for example, have a much nicer coat when some grain is included in the diet and a more sparse coat when grains are entirely omitted.

Grains contain nutrients just as other foods do. Certainly, we can obtain these nutrients from other food sources so if we look at this as the only argument, it would be easy to dismiss grains from the diet altogether. But what do you do when the dog simply isn't able to handle these other foods? For instance, oatmeal contains zinc and we can also provide this mineral through beef tongue, lamb and chicken gizzards, to name three sources. However, the dog that can't eat these meats for one reason or another, may be better off with some oatmeal rather than to be deficient in zinc.

One of the common arguments against the use of grains is that we have to cook or ferment them in order for the dog to be able to utilize the nutrients. It is due to this need for preparation that some people feel that grains are simply not a natural food for canines. And they may be right. If we want to have a philosophical discussion about what may or may not be 'correct' for canines in general, I suppose we could entertain ourselves for quite some time. The fact remains that each dog is an individual and is not always the ideal role model of canine health. While a *diet* may be biologically correct, a *dog* may not be.

We need to feed the diet that works best for the dog(s) we live with. If grains are a part of this scenario, I have no problem with using them. Naturally, I'm not suggesting that the diet be primarily grain, but let's get past the arguments on the subject and feed what the dog shows us is best for *him*.

Weight Gain

Carbohydrates and fat can help a dog to gain weight. I've worked with underweight dogs that could not tolerate fats in sufficient quantity to bulk them up to normal size. Neither could they tolerate enough of the higher calorie vegetables to do the trick. In these cases, grains can help. I am not suggesting that you feed a mountain of grain, but diets that contain ten percent grain to a maximum of fifty percent (and I am not overly pleased with the higher amount) are sometimes needed in the real world.

Vegetables

Dogs do not have the ability to break down the cellulose walls that vegetables contain. Without correctly preparing vegetables for your dog, the nutrients that can be provided by these foods are rendered almost useless. If you'd like proof, try feeding a whole carrot to your pet. Now watch the stool and notice the bits of carrot in it. This is the digestion process at work. The same is true of undercooked grains. Feed some overcooked rice and you're not likely to see any rice in the stool but undercook it and you can almost count the grains.

Vegetables don't need to be cooked as a rule. You can provide the nutrients that vegetables contain in one of two ways. Mechanical breakdown can include putting the raw vegetables through a meat grinder or juicer. If you choose the latter, you can feed the pulp and/or the juice itself. The other option is to cook the veggies. Steaming works nicely but does not break down those stubborn cellulose walls sufficiently. This means that the vegetables will need to be run through a food processor at minimum and the meat grinder at best. The same holds true of totally boiled vegetables although the food processor can do the job in this case.

The nutrients in cooked vegetables may be less than in raw in some cases, but in others, nutrient value goes up. Yes, you read that correctly. Look at the USDA web site[6] and compare the vitamin A content of one cup of cooked carrots to that of one cup of raw carrots. There is quite a bit more vitamin A in the cooked version.

Enzymes and some heat sensitive vitamins are destroyed during the cooking process but minerals and heat stable vitamins are not.

---

[6] http://www.nal.usda.gov/fnic/cgi-bin/nut_search.pl

Does this mean that we should feed only cooked vegetables? No, not at all. But neither does cooking vegetables create a big problem. Some dogs do best on cooked foods while others handle the same food only if it's raw. I've used cooked carrots for example, when I needed to boost the vitamin A content of the diet and the dog couldn't tolerate other foods that are rich in this vitamin. Sometimes, there is a real purpose in using cooked foods.

Some dogs can handle cruciferous vegetables only if they've been steamed. Dogs that tend to have a lot of gas when eating raw broccoli for instance, may not have this reaction if the broccoli is cooked a bit. This is the case for any number of vegetables so if the goal is to feed a variety of foods, you might try steaming some and leaving others in their raw state. See what works for *your* dog.

Cost Factors

Despite the fact that many dogs do beautifully on a totally raw diet, some people use grains to offset the cost of feeding this way. One example that comes to mind is a breeder of Bull Mastiffs. With six huge and hungry dogs in the kennel, this breeder simply could not afford to feed what he preferred to. Adding some grain to the diet made it possible to continue feeding home-prepared foods. Truthfully, I'd rather see this addition of cooked grains than to have all the dogs return to a highly processed diet of commercial dog food.

Real and Imaginary Risks of Cooked Foods

Cooking all ingredients in one pot is convenient. Certainly, many dogs eat a stew-like meal for a lifetime with no ill effects. However, it may be a good idea to cook foods separately from each other.

There are interactions between various dietary components during the cooking process and this interaction can change the structure of amino acids, for example.

Cooked fats may or may not be easily digested by your dog. If you prefer to feed a cooked diet but notice that your pet is having digestive problems, draining the fat may be helpful. Cold pressed oils such as safflower and canola can be added just before feeding time. Some dogs actually react *better* to cooked fats than to raw fats or cold pressed oils. I can't explain why this is so, but my experience tells me that it can happen.

While cooking does destroy bacteria, some people believe that this allows us to become carefree about pathogens in food. Not so! Cooked food can still be contaminated, especially when food is left on the counter for hours on end. Chances are you wouldn't remove roast chicken from the oven and let it sit around for a few hours before serving it to your family, so don't do this with food for your dog. Contamination may come from water, living plants (fruits and vegetables), kitchen equipment, or the food and water bowl that have been left to sit around for hours without being cleaned. When contaminated utensils come into contact with cooked foods, the foods become contaminated as well.

Due to the fact that cooking foods destroys bacteria, some people choose to use vegetables that should have been thrown in the garbage. Rotting foods should never be used whether you feed a raw or cooked diet. Heat does not destroy fungal toxins. I've had clients who thought they were lucky when the grocer gave them vegetables that would otherwise have been discarded. Since dogs are noted for being scavengers, these vegetables were fed to the pets. It was a disaster waiting to happen and it did. You want to feed fresh vegetables to avoid serious toxins but also because you want to provide nutrients that haven't diminished due to spoilage.

Botulism isn't something that most of us think about when feeding a home cooked diet. I had a client who bought cans of vegetables on sale despite the fact that one of these cans seemed to have a bulge in it and smelled 'off' after being opened. While this wasn't something that the human family would want to eat, the dogs didn't seem to mind. As a result, one of the two dogs died. Don't feed your dog something that doesn't look or smell right to you. If in doubt, throw it out!

Enzymes

Some people consider cooked foods to be 'dead' foods and a danger to health due to the lack of enzymes. While it's true that bacteria and enzymes are killed during the cooking process, we need to look a bit deeper in order to understand enzyme activity.

Enzymes are protein molecules that serve as catalysts for biochemical reactions in the body. Without these catalysts, many of these reactions would occur at such a slow pace that sustaining life would be impossible.

Digestive enzymes break down foods into nutrients that the body can absorb. Respiratory enzymes allow for the elimination of carbon dioxide from the lungs. There are many other types of enzymes but by giving you these two examples, you can see why some people divide them into two groups: digestive enzymes and metabolic enzymes. Obviously, we cannot survive without enzymes so 'dead' food sounds as if there's something to worry about. But if that's the case, how did dogs that ate a home cooked diet in years gone by manage to survive at *all*? What happens if your dog simply can't tolerate raw foods?

The body manufactures a supply of enzymes. It can obtain enzymes from food but a healthy body is very capable of producing the enzymes required to keep everything functioning quite well. Some dogs benefit from the addition of digestive enzymes and your vet may guide you as to whether or not this is a requirement. There is more discussion about digestive enzymes in Chapter 12.

Bone Meal

Bone meal provides both calcium and phosphorus in the diet. Ratios and amounts of these two minerals vary depending on the brand you purchase. It is a cooked product.

Some people may point to bone meal as a source of lead or whatever other toxic substance they imagine it holds, but has anyone compared the levels of toxins in bone meal to those in raw, meaty bones? Do we really know the facts about this or are we simply repeating the things we've heard or read about in the past? I would suggest that until the complete analyses on toxins in all bones is made public, we are only guessing. This may lead to interesting arguments but doesn't help the person who needs to make a decision about which calcium source to use.

When I started making food for my dogs, the things I'd read about bone meal scared me. Zoey was already sick enough without adding new problems to her life. She could barely tolerate *food* in those days much less supplements. I did an independent lab analysis on the Swiss Herbal brand of bone meal. It turned out that there were no toxic components to be measured! Laboratory test results can vary so I tested six different bottles of the same brand of bone meal. Yes, I'd become paranoid due to the books that claimed bone meal was dangerous. I can't speak about every bone meal product on the market and it's probably true that brands differ in purity, but all my lab reports stated that the Swiss Herbal brand had untraceable impurities. Knowing that there are pure sources of bone meal can ease your mind. Whether you choose to use it or not is, of course, up to you but I don't accept that it is an 'evil' addition to foods. As a matter of fact, there are times when it's a good option. When the dog does not tolerate another source of calcium and phosphorus in good balance, bone meal can meet the requirements.

Oral Health

Cooked foods are soft in texture and don't allow your dog the opportunity to have an oral workout. Some dogs may require a visit to the vet for a dental cleaning if only cooked foods are fed. Surprisingly though, this is not the case for *all* dogs. There are dogs that eat a raw diet, which allows for ample opportunity to have clean teeth, yet not all of these animals will be able to avoid needing dentistry work. Although I have no studies to present, I believe that at least a part of the picture is genetic make up. Another possibility is medications that may have been needed for lengthy periods of time. Some of these medications impair absorption of calcium regardless of what you feed or how you prepare it.

Summary

- Many dogs thrive on home cooked diets.

- There are situations when cooked diets may be preferable to raw diets: gastric upsets, pancreatitis, required weight gain for a dog that is intolerant of fats, compromised immune systems.

- Grains must be thoroughly cooked. They provide nutrients that a dog may require when he is unable to eat other foods that contain the same nutrients.

- Some dogs digest cooked vegetables more easily than raw vegetables.

- Grains reduce the cost of the diet and may be helpful in situations where someone is attempting to accommodate the needs of several animals while on a budget.

- A normal, healthy body is a marvel at enzyme production and is very good at providing the enzymes required at the appropriate times.

- Cooked foods may not give a dog the opportunity to exercise teeth and gums.

- Fungal toxins are not affected by the cooking process.

- Cooking destroys bacteria but foods may still be contaminated through kitchen utensils and poor hygiene.

Chapter 8

THE MIDDLE GROUND

There are many reasons why some people may opt for combining both raw and cooked foods. The following may help you feel more comfortable about making a decision as to how to feed your dog(s).

If the idea of bacteria in raw meat seems overly frightening or if your dog doesn't tolerate raw meats, you might choose to cook the meat but feed raw vegetables instead. Remember that you need to break down the cellulose walls of vegetables (see Chapter 6).

The length of time you cook meats is something to consider as well. Some dogs do very well with meats that are lightly poached and quite rare on the inside. If bacteria concerns you, plunging the meat into boiling water for a few seconds eliminates *surface* bacteria.

Grains must be cooked for a long time in order for your pet(s) to be able to digest them. You might choose to feed raw meats and vegetables with the addition of cooked grains.

Vegetables can, of course, be fed raw if suitably prepared. However, some dogs simply cannot tolerate vegetables unless they are steamed or cooked all the way through.

Given the options of raw diets, cooked diets or combining the two, making a decision as to which way to feed might seem a bit overwhelming at first. The following scenarios and suggestions may help you to take the initial step towards feeding a home-prepared diet. These are situations that clients bring to me on a daily basis.

Problems and Suggestions

Symptoms experienced by a dog can be due to any number of health problems. Various health conditions call for different diets. Always ensure that your dog has seen the veterinarian and that there isn't a more serious underlying cause for symptoms.

Problem: Your dog is healthy and could probably thrive on a raw diet but you just can't talk your self into feeding this way.

Suggestion: Feed cooked meats with suitably prepared raw vegetables and little or no grain. As you become more comfortable with the whole idea of home-prepared diets, you might decide to cook the meats less and less until they are rare rather than totally raw.

Problem: Your dog has always eaten pet food and has a tendency toward diarrhea and/or vomiting.

Suggestion: Many dogs fare much better on home-prepared meals. To begin with, keep the foods very simple by choosing one meat and one root vegetable. I'm partial to using sweet potatoes or turnips. It is always easier to note allergies when the diet doesn't contain too much variety because you can point to the food culprit faster. Grains can be a problem for dogs that have been on pet food for a long time since most commercial foods are grain-based. These animals may have developed an allergy to grains in general or just one in particular. Keep a diary and make note of the foods that seem to agree with your dog as well as those which are a problem. Build the diet 'up' by adding a supplement (see Chapter 12) and wait 2-8 weeks before adding any other item to the diet. Waiting a full eight weeks is optimal. Some dogs manage best on raw foods while others tolerate the same food items only when they have been cooked. Both diarrhea and vomiting can be due to the body's inability to digest fats, or be associated with other problems. Choose lean meats at first and test this theory out by adding *small* amounts of fat to the diet. These may be in the form of animal fat, such as chicken skin, or cold pressed oils that can be added to the food.

I cannot emphasize enough the need to increase fat content *slowly*. A dog that is predisposed to pancreatitis can be thrown right over the edge if you feed too much fat. For a dog with symptoms as noted above, I would use lightly poached lean meats and work toward a raw diet if that is the goal. Cooked diets may be very well tolerated as well. I would not use raw meaty bones at this time but may decide to introduce them slowly later on, and they would be ground rather than fed whole.

A dog that displays signs of gastrointestinal problems usually needs a more gentle approach than whole bones offer. A calcium supplement such as bone meal or egg shells would be advised. A multi vitamin is also advisable while you take your time and work through a variety of food introductions.

Problem: You want to feed a raw diet but your dog seems to get diarrhea from raw meaty bones.

Suggestion: Use skinless chicken or turkey necks rather than parts that include the skin. Turkey necks are lean and many grinders can manage them. Some dogs can't tolerate too much fat and this may cause them to produce stools that are loose and/or full of mucus. If this doesn't work, consider using bone meal or egg shells in lieu of raw, meaty bones.

Problem: You want to feed a raw diet but your dog becomes ill after eating raw foods - no matter how you prepare them.

Suggestion: Listen to your dog! He knows his own body much better than you ever will. Feed a cooked diet and if you absolutely *must* wean to raw, do it later. There is no point in forcing your dog to eat things that obviously disagree with him. Books or people may tell you that he will be healthier for it, but the dog is trying to tell you something. Give him the last word and respect his individuality and unique needs.

Problem: Your dog has cancer and various people you speak to have different ideas about what the optimal diet should be.

Suggestion: Studies show that diets low in carbohydrates, moderate in protein, and higher in fat, especially the Omega 3 fatty acids, starve cancer. You can prepare foods that meet these goals whether you choose to feed a cooked or raw diet.

Some people feel that raw foods are optimal and dogs with cancer need to be fed this way in order to boost the immune system. This can be a catch-22 because the immune system is already in trouble if cancer is present. With a weakened immune system (especially after treatments such as chemotherapy), the dog may not be able to handle bacteria. In my experience, cooked foods are a great starting point. The fact that you provide fresh and varied foods rather than processed pet foods is already a nutritional bonus.

Once your dog seems to be doing well on a cooked diet you might decide to wean him to a raw diet if that is your preference. Remember that the ability to overcome bacteria is highly dependant on a strong immune system. Dogs with cancer lack this advantage. My choice would be to use cooked meats and raw vegetables.

Problem: Your dog seems to fall victim to worms or mites or is generally a weaker animal than what you consider to be optimal. You tend to spend a lot of time at the vet for one ailment or another.

Suggestion: Starting off with a cooked diet might be the way to go when a dog is obviously not very healthy. Giving the body a chance to mend and strengthen immune response might make more sense than forcing the animal to respond to the challenges of parasites or bacteria. Slowly introducing new foods and watching for positive reactions such as a firm stool, less scratching around sensitive areas, and a general improvement in energy level would be my preference. Once the dog shows that he tolerates the new diet, you can easily switch him to a raw version if that is your choice.

Problem: Your dog has ongoing yeast infections.

Suggestion: Both cooked and raw diets are an option in this case. Yeast is a normal resident of ears and skin but takes over when there is a primary problem. Addressing nutrition responsive diseases causes the yeast to calm down.

Many people seem to be confused about yeast in connection to carbohydrates. It took me some time to understand it as well. Allegations of yeast feeding on carbohydrates are popular myths.

There is no direct connection to carbohydrates and yeast. Yeast feeds on simple glucose just as other organisms do. Carbohydrates are converted into glucose, as are fats. Addressing the underlying problem that has caused a weakened immune system should be the goal. Food allergies or any number of other things can cause yeast to proliferate. Here are two food examples, although the yeast overgrowth may not have a dietary connection to begin with.

Allergies to gluten, for instance, may be resolved by feeding rice rather than oats or other grains that contain gluten. In turn, the yeast problem is likely to disappear. The allergy may be to a variety of meat instead. In this instance, removing the offending meat source from the diet results in better health, which in turn helps the body to keep the yeast at bay.

So it is the underlying problem that needs to be addressed rather than the amount of carbohydrates. If the dog happens to have a gluten allergy and grains are omitted, it is probable that the pet owner will notice improvement in the dog. This shouldn't be confused with the notion that carbohydrates are evil.

Zoey was a challenge when it came to yeast. Her ears were full of yeasty debris and she also had it in her lip folds and around her vulva. The answer for Zoey was to include a probiotic (acidophilus and bifidus) as part of the supplements that she received daily. This helped her very quickly. In addition, I began to sprinkle an herb called Pau D'arco into her food once a day. Finally, I added two drops of grapefruit seed extract to the drinking water. The yeast was under control within six weeks. You might want to speak to your veterinarian before using any of the things I've mentioned. Some dogs are very sensitive to herbs. Grapefruit seed extract is extremely bitter although using just 2 drops in 10 ounces of water didn't seem to bother my dogs in the least. If you add the extract to water, ensure that your dog is drinking well. Some dogs may refuse their water and become dehydrated.

I also used a combination of fifty percent apple cider vinegar and fifty percent witch hazel to clean her ears. This combination works to provide acidity, which is something that yeast isn't partial to. It is also an astringent, which may help inflammation. Keep in mind that both of these items can irritate an area if there is an open sore. I would never use this inside the ear or on an open cut. This was used only to wipe the ear flaps and the visible part of the ear itself.

Problem: Your dog becomes constipated fairly often.

Suggestion: Both cooked and raw diets can work in this situation but be careful not to overdo the raw, meaty bones as part of a raw diet. Since bones tend to firm up stool, you don't want to risk impaction. Feed these with a plan in mind and there shouldn't be any worries, but if you get carried away and feed these as the *greater* part of the diet, you might run into problems.

Use as much as fifty percent vegetables in the diet and make sure that a fair amount is in the green, leafy category if root vegetables tend to produce firm stool. Ensure that your dog is drinking well. Water helps to flush the stool out of the body. If the pet is not a big drinker, adding a bit of water to the food can be helpful. Olive oil and flaxseed oil are especially good for softening stool.

Problem: Your dog has urine pH problems.

Suggestion: Certain breeds are more prone to urine pH problems and have a tendency toward oxalate or struvite crystals. Diets that are high in meat content tend to produce urine that's more acidic.

Adding vitamin C to the diet can create acidic urine. When urine is too acidic, there is a greater chance of oxalate stones developing.
Adding some grain to the diet can help to create urine that's more alkaline. Feeding white meats such as chicken, or fish and eggs, as well as ricotta cheese (providing the dog can handle cheese to begin with) has always helped me when the need for more alkaline urine existed. When urine is concentrated, it can also lead to a greater risk

of stone formation. Ensuring that your dog is drinking well is one of the keys to dilute urine. Again, if the dog is not tempted to drink much, the addition of some good quality water to his food can be very helpful.

Problem: Your dog needs to lose weight.

Suggestion: Both a raw or cooked diet can work towards weight loss but raw, meaty bones can be fairly high in calories due to the fat content. Turkey necks offer a leaner option and a good calcium to phosphorus ratio. A diet may provide enough calories to maintain weight yet leave the dog feeling overly hungry. This is not unlike you or I eating a chocolate bar, which provides plenty of calories but doesn't provide us with a feeling of fullness a few hours later.

A very hungry dog is more apt to gulp food. Keep this in mind if you choose to feed whole bones, and keep an eye on your pet. If raw meaty bones are not offered, cooked or raw foods must have calcium supplementation through bone meal, generic calcium or eggshells. By using a calcium source other than the fatty raw meaty bones (turkey necks may still be a good option), you can eliminate quite a few calories and still provide enough food so that the dog isn't overwhelmed with hunger. Additional fiber in the diet is also helpful. Extra vegetables provide a feeling of fullness without adding many calories.

Problem: Your dog seemed to be doing well on a home-prepared diet but is having a setback now.

Suggestion: Naturally, this depends on the setback in question and hopefully, you've seen your veterinarian to ensure that there isn't anything serious to concern yourself with.

The most common setbacks that I deal with are those of *new* problems seeming to crop up. This is an excellent time to look at the diet for nutrient content and consider some of the possible mineral interactions. To give you a few examples, skin problems may respond to the addition of Omega 3 in the diet (see chapter 12) but could just as easily have to do with insufficient zinc. Skeletal problems may be due to an excess or insufficiency of calcium, but could also be due to an excess or insufficiency of vitamin D. Gastrointestinal problems may be due to the fiber content of the diet or to too much fat.

Review the NRC recommendations (see Chapter 6) and compare the nutrient content of your chosen diet to them. I've found that this is the simplest way to fix many unsolved problems, and what's equally important is that they seem to remain solved. Take your time and note the dog's reactions. In other words, the diet may meet the NRC guidelines but your dog may or may not be *absorbing* the nutrients at the rate you expect. It is the *dog* that needs to guide you.

You can try to increase or decrease certain nutrient values in very small amounts to test the dog's reaction, and adjust the diet accordingly. In my experience, deviating too much from NRC guidelines becomes problematic in the long run, but the source of nutrients is also important. A dog may not always be able to absorb the calcium from eggshells as well as from bone meal. Another dog may be the exact opposite or do best with raw, meaty bones. Yet another may not tolerate bones at all and benefit from generic calcium such as calcium citrate.

Problem: Food allergies

Suggestion: In veterinary circles it is believed that very few dogs actually suffer from food allergies. This is of little importance to the dog guardian who is living with an animal that constantly scratches herself, chews paws, vomits and has diarrhea. Call it an allergy or an adverse response, the bottom line is that this dog needs relief!

There are blood tests to determine food allergies but every veterinarian I've ever spoken to has agreed that these tests are almost worthless. Home-prepared diets are very beneficial in discovering what the food culprit(s) might be. Foods can be cooked or raw.

Interestingly, some dogs react well to the same food when it is fed cooked rather than raw, while others are the exact opposite. Elimination diets work extremely well but positive results are achievable only if the dog guardian follows the plan.

Unfortunately, most people seem to panic on behalf of their dogs when I tell them that the diet will consist of one protein and one vegetable or grain. The immediate response is "But this isn't a balanced diet, is it?" No, it is not. But neither is it a problem for an otherwise healthy adult dog because we have to remember that s/he has accumulated reserves of nutrients in the storage houses of the body (see Chapter 6). There is little, if any risk to feeding just two foods for eight weeks or so and this is the length of time that is usually required. If the dog reacts adversely, switch proteins. Once you find the two foods that seem to be well tolerated, stick with them as you begin to supplement the diet (see Chapter 12). Use each supplement for a few weeks as you wait for an adverse response. Should this happen, eliminate the new addition to test things out.

If the dog becomes well after a few days (it can take as long as six weeks for sensitive dogs to return to normal), try another supplement. You may opt to use a multi vitamin/mineral complex instead. This can work but keep in mind that dogs can react to these as well. The key is to keep it simple and be methodical in your approach.

It is rare for me to find a client who is willing to do what it really takes to discover the possible food culprits that a dog reacts to. Once they calm down long enough to understand that an 'unbalanced' diet for a short period of time is not a big problem, we move on to the next question which is " But what about treats? " This is by far the biggest problem for pet guardians to overcome. The dog begs for her daily ration of biscuits or foods that have always been considered treats and everyone in the household caves in. They don't often tell me that they've sneaked in a dog biscuit, but it's not difficult to tell because inevitably, the original symptoms return. What some people fail to understand is that they are only cheating the dog. The treat might have set this animal back by days or weeks. Finally, the dog guardian becomes frustrated.

My warning to you is that if you are not prepared to go through the diet elimination process properly, be prepared to live with a dog that continues to be miserable. There is no middle ground when it comes to this approach. I assure you that it works remarkably well but you have to be willing to go through the process.

Problem: 'Detox'

The idea of detoxification is becoming increasingly popular. It is sometimes said that once the body is in the process of becoming healthier, it cleans itself of toxins. An example of this process would be someone who quits smoking. While this is a big step towards better health, many people begin to cough and eliminate phlegm despite the fact that they may not have had this occur while smoking. Other people may have headaches or feel generally weaker for a short while. The symptoms of detoxification, are said to be varied.

Perhaps this is why so many people claim that the dog is 'going through detox' when they see mucus in the stool, excessive shedding, vomiting, or any number of symptoms. Certainly, many of my clients believed that detoxification was behind the problems their dogs experienced, and their friends were quick to assure them there was nothing to worry about. The dog was simply getting healthier and all these reactions would stop soon.

I will admit to not being particularly keen on the 'diagnosis' of detoxification. Perhaps it is because my experiences include problems that have nothing to do with a dog becoming healthier. In fact, most of these dogs had been suffering for quite some time before I began to work with them. If the same dog that had mucus in his stool had not been eating a new diet, would the owner have thought that the dog was going through a good experience? If this dog had lost half her coat, would the owner have thought this was normal? When we are eager to see the new diet working well, we sometimes ignore the obvious.

A dog can have mucus in the stool for any number of reasons. Parasites are one possibility. Parasites are sometimes difficult to find and more than one fecal sample should be tested if the mucus continues despite a negative test result. I've had several clients who were advised by well meaning friends that mucus was normal but in fact, the pet had worms or Giardia.

Mucus in the stool can also be a sign of inflammation in the digestive tract. This can happen if the new diet is introduced too quickly or if something has irritated the gastrointestinal tract. Either way, it should not last for more than a few days. I've had clients with dogs that excreted mucus in the stool for weeks and sometimes months. A change in diet solved this almost instantly. Don't ignore the signals that your dog is giving you because in many instances, the irritated tract begins to bleed.

Blood in the stool should never be ignored or thought of as 'detox' When you see mucus and then blood in the stool, you're witnessing a situation that has gone from bad to worse. Again, parasites can be the cause of blood in the stool. A very irritated colon can be the reason as well. There are several other reasons for seeing blood and your veterinarian is your best advisor. Also note that a black stool can be this color due to blood. Bright red blood signifies a problem in the lower part of the colon, whereas black blood (seen as a black colored stool) signifies a problem higher up in the digestive tract.

Diarrhea is sometimes considered to be a part of 'detox'. Again, the cause of this problem could be any number of things. Provided there is no bleeding involved, you can fast an otherwise healthy animal for 12-24 hours. Always provide fresh water. I also like to offer a very mild, home made chicken broth, which has had all visible fat removed. A pinch of salt adds needed sodium. Ensure that your dog remains well hydrated. Look closely at the diet that you've fed. It could be that you introduced new foods too quickly but the problem may just as easily be that something in the diet has irritated the digestive tract. Fats and excessive or insufficient fiber tend to be common culprits but a food allergy is also a possibility. Diarrhea should not last for more than a day or two and your dog should be feeling and acting more normal as the hours pass by. If this is not the case, your veterinarian may be able to identify the cause of the problem. Please don't wait too long to speak to your veterinarian. People don't ignore diarrhea when they are plagued with it but sometimes dogs are expected to go through this for weeks on end. It's not only unfair but can be dangerous as dehydration sets in quickly.

My preference in dealing with diarrhea for an otherwise healthy dog is to offer broth for 12-24 hours, followed by a meal of strained baby food that does not contain any vegetables, grains or thickeners such as cornstarch or tapioca. Using a baby food such as chicken and broth seems to work very well. Obviously, if your dog cannot eat chicken, you would choose another meat source such as beef in broth, turkey in broth, etc.

The next meal would be a home-prepared meal of one protein with boiled and mashed white potato or rice. I like to run this mixture through the food processor to end up with a food that isn't unlike the consistency of baby food. This should be a small meal with added broth to ease digestion. As the stool begins to firm up, I decrease the amount of broth and begin to add a small amount of a vegetable that the dog seems to do well with. Providing the stool is looking normal by the third day, I begin to feed the regular diet again.

Excessive flaking of skin, shedding and hot spots have also been labeled as 'detox' by some people. I've seen dogs that shed excessively and replace the old coat with a brilliant new one. However, the process is never a very long one and the shedding seems to happen relatively soon after changing the diet. When skin problems or excessive shedding develop months after a change in diet, I tend to become suspicious of the reasons that might lie behind this. Looking a bit more deeply into the nutrient composition of the diet can make a huge difference.

Ignoring the signals that you see and claiming that all these things are a form of detox can translate into your dog becoming increasingly low in certain nutrients. While this is not always the case, I believe that checking the nutrient values in the diet is a safety measure that we can all do easily. This may be a good time to remind you that most of the values of minerals and vitamins in common foods are available at the USDA web site:

http://www.nal.usda.gov/fnic/cgi-bin/nut_search.pl

Chapter 9
Vitamins And Minerals

Vitamins and minerals are essential to life. Science has never been able to catch up to Mother Nature and as a result we are discovering the benefits of certain nutrients on what seems to be a weekly basis. In fact, it is the *undiscovered* nutrients that may be the key to maintaining optimal health.

I am often asked about the roles of vitamins and minerals. This subject is not fully understood to begin with but even covering the basics would entail a book unto itself. The following is a very short description of the known functions of vitamins and minerals (there are many more functions than room in this book allows) as well as common foods that contain them. Please refer to the USDA web site in order to learn how *much* of a vitamin or mineral a food contains. The food items listed here are valuable but you may still need or want to know the actual amount of a given vitamin or mineral in a food or diet as a whole. Note that the order of foods listed is not indicative of higher to lower concentrations of the vitamin or mineral.

Vitamin	Function	Foods
Vitamin A (Beta carotene is a Vitamin A precursor)	Enhances immune function, prevents night blindness, aids in formation of bones, antioxidant	Fish liver oils, animal livers, carrots, cantaloupe, spinach, yellow squash, kelp
Vitamin B1 (thiamine)	Brain function, digestion, energy, appetite	Egg yolks, liver, brown rice, poultry, parsley, broccoli
Vitamin B2 (riboflavin)	Healthy skin, metabolism of fats, proteins, carbohydrates	Egg yolks, fish, poultry, meat, broccoli, nuts
Vitamin B3 (niacinamide)	Function of nervous system, healthy skin	Eggs, fish, carrots, beef liver, alfalfa
Vitamin B5 (pantothenic acid)	Fat, protein and carbohydrate metabolism	Eggs, brewer's yeast, beef, kidney, whole wheat
Vitamin B6 (Pyridoxine)	Taurine and carnitine synthesis, promotion of red blood cell formation	Chicken, eggs, meat, potatoes, bananas, whole grains, cantaloupe, spinach
Vitamin B12 (Cobalamin)	Cell formation, supports nerve structure	Kidney, liver, eggs, kelp, brewer's yeast
Biotin	Healthy skin, utilization of other B vitamins	Poultry, eggs, meat, whole grains, brewer's yeast
Choline	Neurotransmitter	Meat, eggs
Folic Acid	Methionine synthesis, proper function of red blood cells	Chicken, beef, lamb, whole grains, raw, green leafy vegetables
Vitamin C	Antioxidant, enhances iron absorption, tissue growth and repair	Citrus fruits, asparagus, spinach, alfalfa, broccoli
Vitamin D	Bone mineralization, proper absorption of calcium and phosphorus	Fish liver oils, egg yolks, oatmeal, butter, alfalfa
Vitamin E	Membrane integrity, antioxidant	Eggs, brown rice, oatmeal, organ meats, alfalfa
Vitamin K	Normal blood coagulation	Egg yolks, alfalfa, liver

Note: If the soil itself is deficient in a mineral, the food grown in this soil may also be deficient.[7]

Mineral	Function	Foods
Boron	Metabolism of calcium, phosphorus & magnesium	Grains, green leafy vegetables, nuts, carrots
Calcium	Constituent of teeth and bones, muscle function	Sardines with bones, green, leafy vegetables
Chromium	Glucose tolerance	Meat, chicken, eggs
Copper	Bone formation, pigmentation, immune function	Liver, oats, salmon, green leafy vegetables, beef, garlic
Iodine	Normal function of thyroid gland	Kelp, saltwater fish, asparagus, garlic
Iron	Production of hemoglobin, oxygenation of red blood cells	Liver, poultry, eggs, fish, whole grains, vegetables, alfalfa
Magnesium	Mineral metabolism, increases calcium uptake	Meat, fish, brown rice, bananas, kelp, alfalfa
Molybdenum	Nitrogen metabolism, cell function	Green leafy vegetables, whole grains, legumes
Phosphorus	Constituent of teeth and bone, energy production	Meat, poultry, eggs, fish, garlic, whole grains
Potassium	Osmotic balance, muscle contraction, transmission of nerve impulses	Poultry, bananas, meat, brewer's yeast, potatoes, brown rice, winter squash
Selenium	Immune function, antioxidant	Chicken, broccoli, kelp, liver, whole grains
Silicon	Healthy skin, nails, hair	Leafy green vegetables, whole grains, alfalfa
Sodium and Chloride	Osmotic pressure, excretion of waste	All foods to some extent. Table salt provides both minerals
Zinc	Protein synthesis, skin health, wound healing	Egg yolks, lamb liver, sardines, meats, grains

---

[7] Worthington V. Nutritional Quality of Organic Versus Conventional Fruits, Vegetables and Grains. J Alt Compl Med 2001; 7(2):161-173

Chapter 10
AMINO ACIDS

In order for a food to be considered valuable, it must provide what the body requires and be properly digested so that absorption of nutrients can occur. Obviously, it must also be palatable, because the most wholesome food is worthless if the animal refuses to eat it.

Proteins are crucial to life. Muscles, glands, organs, tendons, nails, bone growth and other body parts and functions are dependent on proteins. Due to the importance of proteins, it is helpful to understand why amino acid profiles are important as well.

Proteins are chains of amino acids that are linked together. The amino acids present and the order in which they are linked, defines the unique profile of each protein.

Each protein in the body serves a specific need and is not interchangeable with other proteins.

Proteins are therefore crucial and in order for them to be available, the correct amino acids must be available. Mother Nature is very wise and the body manufactures some of these amino acids. It is also capable of combining some amino acids to create others. Of the list of amino acids, those that the body can supply are called *unessential* amino acids. The *essential* amino acids must be supplied through diet. The body is incapable of providing them.

The body has an amino acid bank. The bank stores amino acids that may not be required today but could be needed tomorrow. As a result, the body is able to withdraw amino acids as required and quickly build proteins for new cells or whatever needs arise. As in the case of mineral stores, it is crucial that the bank does not run out of essential amino acids. Should even one essential amino acid be missing, the body cannot continue normal protein synthesis.

When we discuss foods that are a good protein source, some people think this refers to the *amount* of protein in the food. That is only a part of the picture. We also want to focus on the amino acid profile within the proteins that a food offers.

Classifications of Amino Acids:

Essential	Non-essential
Argine	Alanine
Histadine	Asparagine
Isoleucine	Aspartic Acid
Leucine	Cysteine
Lysine	Glutamic Acid
Methionine	Glutamine
Phenylalanine	Glycine
Threonine	Proline
Tryptophan	Serine
Valine	Tyrosine

You may look at this list and notice that some amino acids seem to be missing. For example, taurine is noted for heart health and other important roles. Taurine is one of the most abundant *free* amino acids in the body and is produced by combining other amino acids. Cats may not have the ability to do this well but dogs have no problem in this regard. If you are concerned about providing a dietary source of taurine, look to meat, eggs and fish as good sources.

Recent studies point to the need for additional taurine in the canine diet. I admit to being a little perplexed by this. A home-prepared diet may already include taurine, whereas in highly processed dog foods the addition might be required. Still, if in doubt, you may want to add this amino acid. It's easily found in pharmacies and health food stores. The current thinking is to add 250 mg daily for a medium sized dog, 500 mg daily for large breeds and 1 gram per day for giant breeds.

Carnitine has been grouped together with other amino acids but in fact, it is a substance related to the B vitamin group. The main function of carnitine is to transport fatty acids. It is not a part of protein synthesis. It can be manufactured by the body if the amino acids methionine and lysine, as well as sufficient quantities of vitamins B1 and B6, are available. Meats and other foods of animal origin are a good source of carnitine.

Gamma-Aminobutyric Acid is formed in the body from glutamic acid. Since glutamic acid is a nonessential amino acid, there is no need to worry about providing it through diet.

Glutathione is not an amino acid although some people consider it to be. In fact, it is a tripeptide (three amino acids) and is produced in the body from glutamic acid, cysteine, and glycine - all of which are nonessential amino acids.

Since essential amino acids must be derived from food sources, the following should be helpful when you think about putting a diet together for your pet. The name of the amino acid is followed by a few foods that contain it in good quantity. Keep in mind that it is highly unlikely that you would go wrong simply by feeding a variety of foods. There are other amino acids that tend to be used to address certain problems. For instance L-Glutamine has been used with success for dogs that have gastrointestinal problems.

Arginine: meat, dairy products, oats and wheat.

Histadine: rice, chicken, meat and wheat.

Isoleucine: chicken, liver, eggs, fish and almonds.

Leucine: meat, brown rice and nuts.

Lysine: red meats, eggs, fish and potatoes.

Methionine: meat, fish, garlic, and eggs.

Phenylalanine: seeds, dairy and almonds.

Threonine: chicken, eggs, beef, bananas and grains.

Typtophan: poultry, eggs, meat, grains, fish and bananas.

Valine: meat, dairy products and grains.

A food that contains most of the essential amino acids would be considered to be a good quality protein. However, keep in mind that we also need to consider the body's ability to break down foods so these amino acids are easily available. A food that goes through the body and is left almost entirely undigested is of little value. A food that is finally digested after wreaking havoc with compromised organs is obviously not what we strive toward. Therefore the foods that contain essential amino acids must also be easily digested before we can consider them to be a part of optimal nutrition.

The quality of a protein is determined by a variety of methods. We can look at the amounts of essential amino acids in a protein and compare them with the animal's needs but this may too simplistic. There are many interactions between essential amino acids and other substances in the body. The most accurate way of determining protein quality is to feed the protein and see how well the animal uses it. This is referred to as the biological value of a protein. Here are a few basic examples of biological values.[8] Varying sources differ in their evaluation of biological values but everyone seems to agree that eggs are the protein that all others need to be measured against.

Whole egg	93.7
Milk	84.5
Fish	76.0
Beef	74.3
Soybeans	72.8
Rice, polished	64.0
Whole wheat	64.0
Corn	60.0
Beans, dry	58.0

Summary

- A highly valued protein is palatable, easy to digest and offers good quantities of essential amino acids.

- Unessential amino acids are ones that the body can provide.

---

[8] Food and Agriculture Org. of the United Nations. The Amino Acid Content of Foods and Biological Data on Proteins

- Essential amino acids are those that must be provided by foods.

- The body 'banks' amino acids for future use.

- Should even one amino acid be missing, the body is incapable of continuing normal protein synthesis.

- Eggs are considered to be the most perfect protein.

- Different foods provide various amino acids in varying amounts.

Chapter 11
THE ABC'S OF FOODS

Knowing the nutrient content of various foods is a good starting point. Knowing the facts about mineral interactions is helpful. Taking a look at the nutrient requirements of dogs while considering that these requirements are not based on a home-prepared diet, gives us something to think about. Where do you go from here? What sorts of foods can you use?

Dairy Products

Butter provides fat, sodium, potassium and vitamin A as well as calcium and phosphorus in amounts equal to each other. Since it is pure fat, many dogs vomit or have diarrhea after consuming it.

I usually avoid butter in diets for dogs because most of them simply don't tolerate it very well. On occasion, I've incorporated it into a diet that was too lean for one reason or another.

Buttermilk may provide live cultures (although not all do), fat, some vitamin A, vitamin C, selenium, potassium and a good balance of calcium to phosphorus.

Cheese provides some calcium but not always enough to balance the phosphorus it contains. Cottage cheese is an example of this with 100gr providing 60 mg of calcium and 132 mg of phosphorus.

Eggs are *the* protein food that all other proteins are measured against. They provide a very high quality protein, vitamin E, selenium, essential fatty acids, sulfur, lecithin and a host of other minerals. If the chicken is fed flaxseeds, the eggs will be even higher in Omega 3 content. This is a very healthy food and is especially good for dogs with coat and skin problems.

Milk provides a source of calcium that is nicely balanced with phosphorus. It also contains potassium, sodium and can provide some vitamin A and D when it is fortified. Fat content depends on the type of milk used.

I find that many dogs are intolerant to milk.

Yogurt may provide living cultures known as probiotics, fat, protein, calcium and some B vitamins.

It is one of the traditional home remedies for diarrhea although it can actually cause diarrhea if the dog does not tolerate it. This is true of any of food of course, but since yogurt is touted as a 'cure', it is especially important to feed it in small amounts to see how the dog reacts. I know of many people who fed a generous helping of yogurt to stop diarrhea only to discover that their pet became more ill than before this was fed.

Fish

Alaskan Pollack, sardines, turbot and any number of other varieties are available as fresh, frozen or canned fish. Fish containins healthful properties but we need to consider that we live in a changed world.

Our polluted waters have affected the entire planet and that includes fish. Mercury and PCBs are of great concern.

There is an enzyme in raw fish that inhibits the absorption of Vitamin B1. Fish is a good provider of the Omega 3 fatty acids.

Some people feed raw fish to their pets. If this is your preference, keep in mind that Pacific Northwest salmon and trout may carry a rickettsial organism known as Neorickettsia helminthoeca. Aquatic snails serve as intermediate hosts for a fluke that may be infected with this. The fluke leaves the snail and penetrates the tissues of salmonid fish, forming cysts. When a dog eats an infected fish, the flukes are released and become egg-laying adults. When the rickettsia causing salmon disease infect the fluke, they multiply in the dog's lymphatic system, spreading into the blood stream.

Freezing may lower infectivity although I am not aware of it rendering the fluke and bacteria harmless. Symptoms include a high fever with vomiting progressing to diarrhea. While IV and certain drugs can be used to combat the disease, there is risk of death. It is believed that ninety percent of untreated dogs die.

In short, it would be prudent to avoid feeding raw fish from the Pacific Northwest.

Fruits

Most dogs have a sweet tooth and will appreciate a fruit treat. Keep in mind that fruits do not provide any *known* nutrients that cannot be obtained in vegetables. Nevertheless, there is no reason not to give your healthy pet a nibble of fruit. I say a *nibble* because many dogs get a loose stool when too much fruit is offered. Once you see what your dog tolerates, go ahead and offer fruits. Some dogs can digest grapefruits and oranges but many seem to have trouble with these fruits. If you're tempted to offer either of these, I'd suggest that you try only a small piece at first.

The following is a short list of what seems to be the most common fruits fed to dogs.

Apples provide an equal amount of calcium to phosphorus as well as some potassium and vitamin C.

Bananas are valued for their high potassium content. A small banana provides 6 mg of calcium and 29 mg of phosphorus.

Blueberries are fairly high in fiber content and also provide a good source of vitamin C. Twenty five berries would provide 2 mg of calcium and 3.5 mg of phosphorus.

Cantaloupe - just a small wedge of this melon provides a good source of vitamin C and a calcium content of 6 mg with a phosphorus content of 9 mg.

Mango - Half of an average size mango provides 10 mg of calcium, 11 mg of phosphorus, vitamin C and enough vitamin A (3,894 IU) to make this fruit very notable.

Strawberries - one large strawberry contains 2.52 mg of calcium and 3.42 mg of phosphorus. These berries are an excellent source of vitamin C.

Grains

Some people incorporate grains into a diet for their dogs while others will have nothing to do with them. If your dog doesn't tolerate some grains, there's not much to think about as far as what nutrients they contain. However, many dogs eat a variety of grains without problems while others may do well on one particular type of grain. In fact, some dogs thrive when some grain is added to their food. In my experience, gluten allergies are a more common problem than an actual reaction to grain itself. In this case, rice works very well.

For those who *do* want to include grains, the list of options is long. The following includes some information on the grains that are most popular and relatively easy to find. Keep in mind that although I include the protein amount, these are not considered to be high quality proteins.

Many people use grains to provide some selenium, which is why I've made a point of mentioning this mineral here and not in other areas of this chapter. Other foods provide selenium as listed in chapter eight and you can see the exact values on the USDA web site.

There is no study that indicates an established need for carbohydrates in the diet of a non-pregnant dog. For this reason, I also note the amount of carbohydrates in grains. Although I am not advocating grains as the predominant part of the diet, neither have I seen a report that shows a bit of grain to be a problem. In fact, grain has helped some of the dogs that I've worked with over the years.

Barley (100gr, cooked) contains about 2% protein, 28% carbohydrate, some folate and potassium. A 100gr portion provides enough selenium to support the daily needs of a 4 kg dog according to the NRC.

Brown rice (100gr, cooked) contains about 2.5% protein, 23% carbohydrate, some B vitamins, and a small amount of potassium. A 100gr serving provides enough selenium to support the daily needs of a 4 kg dog according to the NRC.

Buckwheat (100gr, cooked) contains about 3% protein, 20% carbohydrate, a small amount of potassium and enough selenium to support the daily need of a 1 kg dog according to the NRC.

White rice (100gr, cooked) contains about 2.5% protein, 28% carbohydrate, some folate and a small amount of potassium. A 100gr serving provides enough selenium to support the daily need of a 3kg dog according to the NRC.

Meat

A variety of meats will provide different nutrients in varying amounts. You can choose to feed it in chunks or grind it yourself. If you feed a cooked diet, the ground meats found in stores are fine because you're killing bacteria through the cooking process. If you choose to feed a raw diet, remember that ground meat may have a higher amount of bacteria in it. In this case, grinding your own meat makes sense because you have control over the hygiene in your own kitchen.

Beef seems to be one of the most common allergens. I suspect (but have no proof) that this may be due to the fact that it is a common bacterial culture medium. If your dog tolerates beef, it is a valuable food because it contains fair levels of zinc.

I'm not partial to beef as the main protein for older dogs or those that suffer from arthritis. The higher levels of arachidonic acid may help to promote inflammation.

Chicken is a popular food for humans so perhaps this is why so many people use this bird as the mainstay of a canine diet. I advise that you not use *any* protein source exclusively unless you also include a multi vitamin/mineral complex. Chicken skin contains a lot of fat, as do the raw, meaty bones. This provides essential fatty acids but I find that a dog eating a diet that is based on chicken usually ends up with flaky skin after a while. The addition of wild salmon oil or flaxseed oil to provide a source of Omega 3 essential fatty acids (see Chapter 11) is usually a good way to combat the problem.

If you cook chicken on the bone, the minerals that were in those bones will leach into the meat and broth to some extent. Raw chicken meat without the bone will provide good protein but be quite low in zinc and iron content.

Duck provides 39gr of fat per 100gr of meat with skin. As you might imagine, it is the skin that increases fat content. The same amount of duck meat alone contains about 6gr of fat. Due to the fatty skin, there are good levels of essential fatty acids but many dogs cannot tolerate the very high fat content.

Goat offers nice iron and zinc content and some B vitamins. This meat varies greatly in fat content. It depends on where the animal was raised and at what age it was slaughtered.

Lamb meat tends to be very fatty and is considered one of the 'rich' foods for this reason. It is a valuable source of zinc and selenium although the selenium content may vary based on where the lamb was raised. Due to the combination of fat and zinc, lamb can be very helpful to dogs with skin problems or dry coats.

Pork contains good levels of essential fatty acids with reasonable amounts of some B vitamins (a good source of niacin).

Rabbit provides a good amount of potassium and zinc as well as essential fatty acids. It is of great value to dogs that suffer from skin and coat problems. As noted in Chapter 5, whole rabbit without the head does not provide much in the way of calcium.

Turkey necks are a great source of calcium and much leaner than chicken necks. This is especially valuable to the raw fed dog that needs to lose weight or does not tolerate fats well. Turkey meat provides high quality protein.

Venison provides a lower amount of fat and therefore fewer calories than beef. It contains higher amounts of iron than poultry, beef, pork and lamb meat. It is a bit higher in cholesterol than the other meats noted and provides a reasonable amount of some B vitamins.

Offal

Many years ago, people ate the various organs and glands of farm animals. Today, most of North America has reserved this practice for different nationalities or expensive restaurants that offer 'sweetbreads' on the Nouvelle Cuisine menu. Your dog is not an elitist and can benefit from these nutritious foods.

Please make certain that the offal you purchase has been federally inspected. This is the safest way of ensuring that the organ meats don't include parasite cysts. The internal organs of most farm animals are a common breeding ground for parasites, which are killed off during the cooking process. If you feed a raw diet, be careful that your source of offal is as free of parasites as possible.

Brains contain a lot of cholesterol and a fair amount of the B vitamins. This combination makes them a valuable food for dogs that tend to have dry skin. They are a food to avoid if your dog has elevated cholesterol levels and your veterinarian advises you to use low cholesterol foods. However, dogs do not normally have problems with elevated cholesterol levels in the way people do.

Hearts provide a good source of B vitamins and iron. They are also a *lean* form of protein that provides some vitamin A.

Kidneys are usually attached to chicken backs or offered in stores as beef and pork kidneys. They provide less vitamin A than liver and good vitamin B and iron content.

Liver is probably the most common organ meat to be fed. Dogs seem to love it and the price makes it quite affordable. Liver is very high in vitamin A content. This is good but can become a problem if too much liver is fed. Vitamin A is a fat-soluble vitamin that is stored in the body. As such, high amounts can become toxic. Lamb liver has exceptionally high vitamin A content. Liver is an excellent way to provide B vitamins as well as selenium and iron.

Lungs are not easily found at supermarkets or butchers. Some ethnic communities may offer these organs at very inexpensive prices. Lungs offer some B vitamins and a relatively small amount of zinc.

Tongue may not be an easy food to find unless you visit a butcher shop. Although it has been listed as offal, I consider tongue to be muscle meat. There is a thick layer of skin that some dogs find difficult to digest when this meat is cooked. Removing it is simply a matter of carving it away with a sharp knife. This layer does not seem to cause a digestive problem when it is raw. Tongue offers protein and some fat much like any other meat, but one of its values is the zinc content. Beef tongue offers a fair amount of zinc and may be a useful part of the diet for a dog that does not tolerate many of the zinc rich foods.

Vegetables

We are very fortunate to have such a vast variety of vegetables available to us throughout the year. It would be almost impossible to note all the different vegetables so I am focusing on the ones that provide almost equal or more, calcium to phosphorus. Of course, vegetables provide far more than these two nutrients. They contain antioxidants, vitamin C, folic acid, vitamin A and fiber, to name only a few important reasons why you want to incorporate them into any diet. We cannot look to vegetables to provide nearly enough calcium and phosphorus in canine diets. However, when you are trying to keep a 'balance' of calcium and phosphorus in a feeding program, the following vegetables and herbs may be of particular interest.

Acorn squash,
raw 100 gr.- calcium 33 mg, phosphorus 36 mg
cooked 100 gr.- calcium 44 mg, phosphorus 45 mg

Butternut squash

raw 100gr.- calcium 48, mg phosphorus 33 mg

cooked 100gr.- calcium 41 mg, phosphorus 27 mg

Celery

raw 100gr. - calcium 40 mg, phosphorus 25 mg

cooked 100gr.- calcium 42 mg, phosphorus 25 mg

Dandelion leaves

raw 100gr.- calcium 187 mg, phosphorus 66 mg

cooked 100gr.- calcium 140 mg, phosphorus 42 mg

Dill

fresh 100gr.- calcium 208 mg, phosphorus 66 mg

dried 100gr.- calcium 1784 mg, phosphorus 543 mg

Green beans (snap)

raw 100gr.- calcium 37 mg, phosphorus 38 mg

cooked 100gr.- calcium 46 mg, phosphorus 39 mg

Leaf lettuce

raw 10gr.- calcium 6.8 mg, phosphorus 2.5 mg

Parsley

raw 1 TBS- calcium 5.24 mg, phosphorus 2.20 mg

dried 1 TBS- calcium 19.08 mg, phosphorus 4.56 mg

Peppermint
fresh, 2 TBS- calcium 7.77mg, phosphorus 2.33mg

Romaine lettuce
raw 10gr.- calcium 3.6 mg, phosphorus 4.5 mg

Spaghetti squash
raw 100gr.- calcium 23 mg, phosphorus 12 mg
cooked 100gr.- calcium 21 mg, phosphorus 14 mg

Spearmint
fresh, 2 TBS- calcium 22.68 mg, phosphorus 6.84 mg
dried, 1 tsp-calcium 7.44 mg, phosphorus 1.38 mg

Turnip
raw 100gr.- calcium 30 mg, phosphorus 27 mg
cooked 100 gr.- calcium 22 mg, phosphorus 19 mg

Watercress
raw 25gr.- calcium 30 mg, phosphorus 15 mg

Organically Grown Foods

Unfortunately, our food sources may be as much a source of illness as a source of nutrition. In an effort to increase production and efficiency as well as profits, we have changed the farming environment and may be harming ourselves in the process.

Animals that are confined to stalls or pens are under a lot of stress, which in turn predisposes them to illness. They are also more likely to become ill from contamination of shared feeding troughs and an environment that is less than clean.

The focus of 'factory' animal farming is to fatten the animal to optimal market weight in as short a period of time as possible while incurring minimal expense. In this situation, a sick animal or herd can become a financial nightmare. Rather than risk illness, farm animals may be vaccinated and medications may be used to address or prevent disease. These practices alone may not be the biggest concern. Perhaps the bigger problem is that some farms use antibiotics in the feed or water troughs on a routine basis. The idea behind this is that the medications may prevent and control outbreaks of infectious diseases in the herd. This is a controversial practice that has gained the attention of many regulators and consumers.

By continually providing antibiotics to an animal that does not require them, we may be creating a problem. Bacteria have the ability to mutate which makes them resistant to more and more medications. When the animal becomes ill and the antibiotics available no longer work to fight off that illness, the disease may run rampant throughout the herd. Furthermore, despite the fact that farm animals are to be free of any medications for three months prior to slaughter, this may not always be the case. The greater concern is when medicated animals shed drug resistant microbes into the environment, including the packaging plants where their meat is processed. These resistant bacteria are then present in the meat that is sold and can cause severe - sometimes fatal - illness in people.

Other than the possible medical problems, there is reason to look at factory farming as inferior for other reasons. Animals that are not raised on natural pastures are rarely, if ever exposed to fresh air and direct sunlight. In my opinion, this is not only a cruel practice but cannot bode well for the nutrient content of the flesh we eat.

We should also consider vegetables, fruits and grains when we look at organically grown foods. Since pesticide residue and genetically modified foods are not inviting, organic produce is gaining the attention of many consumers.

While I don't believe that factory farming can provide optimal nutrition for people, I feel even more strongly about it for pets. Imagine what our animals are exposed to on a daily basis. Car exhaust fumes are right at nose level. Grass full of chemicals that are not only inhaled by a curious nose but also absorbed by the skin on bare paws, and ultimately ingested when the paws are licked. Polluted air, yearly vaccines, chemical cleansers in our homes...pets are not leading a very natural life at the best of times! Feeding a diet that provides foods, which are not laden with chemical residue, seems to be the least we can do.

Having given you my reasons for encouraging the consumption of organically grown foods, it is only fair that I touch upon the possible problems as well.

While these foods are becoming more popular and therefore more accessible, they may not always be available when we'd like them to be. Since fruits and vegetables tend to be seasonal, a great variety may not be available at all times. Butchers and markets may not always have the cut of meat we'd prefer and depending on where you live, these products may be unavailable altogether. To complicate things further, there is no doubt that most of the time, organic products cost more money. Arguments regarding the health benefits seem pointless when the budget simply does not allow us to purchase what we'd prefer.

Hopefully, all of the points above will be addressed as market demand for organic products increases. Farmers and stores may be able to reduce prices while providing availability if more people request organic foods. In the meantime, we can do our best by purchasing *some* organic foods. For instance, organic eggs cost about two dollars more per dozen than regular farmed eggs. That may seem like quite a difference but, in fact, translates to only sixteen cents more per egg. Since the humble egg is such an inexpensive source of perfect protein, it may be the organic food you can afford easily. You, your family and your pets are worth it!

Organic meats come from animals that have been raised naturally. They have not been fed antibiotics or growth hormones. Their feed has been organically grown as well. They may or may not have had access to open pastures. You need to verify details with the grower if you have questions, because there can be differences in how animals are raised from one producer to the next. Some farmers use worming medications while others do not. Animals that have not been wormed may carry more parasites. It is true that an animal raised with less stress is not as likely to develop some illnesses but they can still harbor parasites. Animals are raised for human consumption and the assumption is that the meat will be cooked thoroughly. Organically grown meats provide many benefits, but this does not detract from the possibility of parasites being part of the picture. Organically raised food may be just as full of parasites as farm raised food.

The label claiming 'free range' chicken is appealing because we tend to imagine chickens pecking at seeds as the farmer walks about his sunny field. In fact, despite the chickens being organically raised, they can be free to walk around a barn and not much else. The birds may still be overcrowded and have little access to fresh air or direct sunlight. If what you are searching for are *humanely* raised chickens that feed on organically grown food and have not been given antibiotics or hormones, you want to investigate the grower. Labels can be misleading in any industry.

Water

Our entire planet would die without it, yet many of us continue to take water for granted. Our water is not the way it used to be in grandma's time and this has created a new industry. Bottled and filtered waters are in almost every grocery store we enter. Many people consider tap water to be a detriment to our health.

Depending on where you live, tap water may indeed be chock full of very nasty things. Have you had your water tested? Maybe you should. It can contain any number of toxins and parasites. Enough so, that many of us are buying water from specialty stores. On a positive note, your water supply may be fine. I'd still look into it, though.

The label that tells you that bottled water comes from a spring is fairly meaningless. It doesn't mean that the spring was clean or that it provides any benefits over your tap water.

Mineral water is a mystery. Which minerals does it contain and where did it come from?

Distilled water has many claims attached to it. Some people believe that it leaches inorganic minerals out of the body. If this is so, I applaud it. However, others believe that it also leaches the good/required minerals out of the body. If in fact that's true, we have a problem. Still, I know many people who have been drinking distilled water for well over ten years and are doing just fine.

My personal choice has been reverse osmosis water. However, as I continue to look for information, I sometimes come across something that makes me stop and think things over again.

A book by Paavo Airola[9] discusses the risks involved with purified waters and Dr. Zoltan Rona [10] seems to have valid arguments against it. To detoxify the body of heavy metals, it seems that purified waters make a lot of sense. However, on an ongoing basis, it may indeed cause problems because these waters are absorptive in nature due to lacking minerals. As a result they may also be rather aggressive in their absorption of the minerals they come into contact with. According to Dr. Rona (past president of the Canadian Holistic Medical Assoc. with a Master's Degree in Biochemistry and Clinical Nutrition from the University of Bridgeport in Connecticut), water filtered through a solid charcoal filter is slightly alkaline and ozonation of this charcoal filtered water is ideal for daily drinking.

Why do we need to search for the best water possible? Frankly, because our water supply today is a mess. Some people have poor quality drinking water available to them in their own homes. Providing water, the most basic and important nutrient in life, should also mean that we provide something that is not full of chemicals or worse.

---

[9] Airola, P. 1974 How To Get Well, Phoenix AZ health Plus Publishers
[10] Rona, Zoltan P. and Martin, Jeanne Marie. Return to the Joy of Health, Vancouver: Alive Books, 1995.
Rona, Zoltan P. Childhood Illness and The Allergy Connection. Rocklin, California:Prima Books, 1996

Summary

- Yogurt is a traditional home remedy for diarrhea but as some dogs are intolerant of yogurt, it is best to feed a small amount at first.

- Raw fish contains an enzyme that impairs absorption of vitamin B1.

- Raw salmonid fish from the Pacific Northwest carries a rickettsial organism that can be deadly to your dog.

- Many vegetables offer a good ratio of calcium to phosphorus. The use of these vegetables in the canine diet provides variety and easy to manage balance of these two minerals.

- Organically grown foods provide wonderful nutrition with an emphasis on maintaining natural soil conditions without the use of chemicals.

- Organically raised animals are not given antibiotics or hormones.

Chapter 12
SUPPLEMENTS

At the risk of giving away my age, I remember when pharmacies didn't offer much more than the filling of a prescription from my doctor. There were always a few sundry items on the shelves but not like today! And health food stores? Those usually offered some mysterious supplements while incense burned and sitar music played in the background.

Today, supplements have become mainstream and new ones seem to pop up almost weekly. We find them in our supermarkets and pharmacies and are overwhelmed by them at the health food stores. Every company has something 'better' or 'new and improved'. It can be difficult to make sense of any of it at the best of times. Even more confusing is the information that we try to gather when, in fact, not very much is known about some of these items.

Science tends to disprove things rather than prove them. All we have to do is look back and remember when we were told that butter was going to kill us all. Then margarine came to the rescue. But wait! It depends on what kind of margarine. Don't buy the hard ones. Apparently those will kill you too. A few years later, margarine was said to be as bad if not worse than butter. Today, butter is supposedly fine as long as we don't use too much of it. So how much is *too* much?

Do you remember when we were advised to take plenty of vitamin C daily? Lately, research is pointing to the 'fact' that vitamin C in excess works as a pro-oxidant rather than an anti-oxidant. So what exactly is 'excess'? What are we supposed to believe? It can be very confusing to say the least!

I think that Mother Nature provides all the answers. We just don't listen very well sometimes. Nor can we understand what is in front of us much of the time. If it's bountiful in nature, maybe we need it and if it's hard to find, maybe we don't need too much of it. Sound simple? Maybe so, but what are the chances of Mom Nature placing a being on the planet without also providing the nutrients to sustain that creature? Emotional arguments aside, the fact is that some of us, including our pets, cannot tolerate the very foods that are supposed to nourish us. That's where supplements come in.

B Vitamins

Dogs manufacture B vitamins. Keep in mind that these are water-soluble vitamins, which means they are excreted through urine. A steady supply of B vitamins is crucial but B-12 lasts longer in the body than the others. It is recycled as well as being manufactured by some of the intestinal bacteria. Your dog will excrete excess B vitamins so there is little risk when using a supplement, although you would not want to give a Chihuahua a human dose. Common sense would tell us this. Expect the urine to be a bright shade of yellow. Never use a particular B vitamin without the advice of your veterinarian. A multi B is safer because the B group works synergistically. Too much niacin (vitamin B3) can cause a rash and/or itch. This reaction disappears quickly as the body excretes excess amounts.

Giving a multi B supplement on an empty stomach can cause nausea and vomiting. Always give it *with* food.

I usually use a multi B vitamin for dogs that do not tolerate foods that provide enough of these, or for those with skin and/or digestive problems. Commonly, the dosage is 12.5 mg for a dog weighing under 25 pounds, 25 mg for 24-40 pounds and anywhere from 30-50 mg for dogs weighing more. Much depends on the diet itself. Generally, I supplement with a multi B complex vitamin 2-3 times per week if the diet is fairly rich in these vitamins and daily if the diet is poor in them.

Vitamin C

This is perhaps *the* vitamin that I'm asked about most. It's touted as almost a cure-all and many people add it to their pet's food 'just in case'. I'm not a big believer in 'just in case' and this is why:

While it's true that vitamin C is water-soluble, this does not mean that there is no chance of it causing a problem. Vitamin C can upset the stomach although there are versions of it, such as ester-C, that are far less likely to cause this reaction. Nevertheless, you might not want to use much C for a dog suffering from gastrointestinal woes.

Other than gastric upset, vitamin C can also acidify urine. When we *want* to accomplish this, C comes in quite handy. However, when the urine is already fairly acidic, acidifying it further can predispose the pet to urinary tract problems such as crystals/stones. Another potential problem is that vitamin C works with gastrin from the stomach to increase calcium absorption. Excess calcium is excreted in the urine along with excess vitamin C, which is excreted as oxalic acid. Calcium and oxalate equals potential crystal formation. This is especially true in acid urine.

Dogs manufacture their own vitamin C. This vitamin is also found in fruits and vegetables. A home-prepared diet does not require supplementation with this vitamin unless there is a specific purpose in doing so. A vet who is well versed in nutrition is your best advisor. There are health problems that can be helped by vitamin C but using it on a whim can backfire on you.

Vitamin E

This is a great antioxidant and every dog should have it included in the diet. When you read labels, you will come across two forms of this vitamin - dl-alpha tocopherol and d-alpha tocopherol. It is the *d-alpha* version that is best absorbed and most potent. Note that the great majority of vitamin E supplements on the market are derived from soy. In my experience, soy tends to be one of the common allergens for dogs. It also tends to be a genetically modified product these days. If you prefer to use a product that does not contain soy, simply look for this vitamin in a soy free version. I've known many itchy dogs that benefited from a soy free supplement.

Depending on the diet, I generally use about 10 IU of vitamin E per pound of body weight.

Kelp

A popular addition to home made diets, kelp is a sea plant that is usually available in a powdered, tablet, or granulated form. It provides a rich source of minerals and some B vitamins. One of the minerals that kelp contains is iodine. Dogs require iodine just as we do, but you can overdo a good thing. There are books that instruct you as to how much kelp should be used within a diet. That might be appealing and seems to take the guesswork out of things but I urge you not to take these recommendations literally.

A *variety* of dried sea plants are sold as kelp. The iodine content between them varies dramatically. It is impossible for anyone to tell you how much kelp is ideal unless you know the iodine content of the kelp you purchase. When I asked for laboratory assays from three kelp producers, there wasn't *one* that was remotely close in iodine content to the next.

Keep in mind that kelp also provides a small amount of protein. Due to this, some dogs may display allergic reactions. Sometimes, people look for the source of a food reaction and focus on the main components of the diet, but a supplement is just as likely to be the culprit.

Kelp is a good source of minerals but you must know the nutrient content and ensure that the kelp comes from as clean a body of water as possible.

Alfalfa Powder

This is a mineral rich food that is a wonderful addition to your dog's diet. I prefer the powdered form to tablets since most dogs do not take well to swallowing pills of any kind.

Alfalfa varies in nutrient content depending on the time of year that it is harvested. In the spring, it contains more moisture and less fiber. As the plant ages during the summer and finally becomes 'old' in the autumn, the fiber content rises. This is one of the reasons why some dogs can suddenly seem to be intolerant of alfalfa. It is not usually the plant itself that is causing the problem, but rather the sudden increase in fiber content.

Good quality alfalfa is organic or wild-crafted. It is not sprayed with chemicals. It should also smell fresh. You can identify a quality alfalfa by the pleasant, grassy odor and a fairly bright green color. When you see a dark brown alfalfa powder, consider it to have been harvested later in the year and far more likely to contain a good deal of fiber.

Kelp and Alfalfa Combinations

Due to the fact that both of these items contain certain nutrients, some people use a combination of the two to provide minerals. Keep in mind that although something may contain a certain mineral, it does not necessarily mean that it provides *enough* of it. For instance, alfalfa provides some zinc but you would have to feed a kilogram of alfalfa to provide the bare minimum amount of zinc for a sixty pound dog.

Commonly, we see an impressive list of nutrients when we look at what kelp and alfalfa contain. Consider the following:

Vitamin A, B complex, biotin, vitamin C, choline, chromium, copper, vitamin D, vitamin E, fiber, folic acid, inositol, iodine, iron, vitamin K, magnesium, manganese, molybdenum, phosphorus, protein, selenium, silicon, sodium, sulfur, and zinc.

Wow! This seems perfect. However, perhaps we should ask what *quantities* of each nutrient does this provide? As an adjunct to a good diet, both kelp and alfalfa can be valuable. However, we need to consider the entire diet rather than hope that mineral requirements are met in these powdered forms.

Salt

Some people have an aversion to the addition of salt to the diet. The fact is that in the correct amount, salt provides sodium and iodine, which are essential nutrients. Kelp provides sodium and iodine as well as other nutrients, but since some dogs cannot tolerate kelp, simple table salt is a viable option. The key is to use it wisely. One half teaspoon of iodized table salt provides about 100 mg of iodine, although this can vary. You might know more details if you ask the manufacturer of the particular brand that you purchase.

Probiotics

Lactobacillus acidophilus, bifidus and a host of other probiotics are available at health food stores as well as some pharmacies. When we use probiotics, we are 'seeding' the digestive tract with beneficial bacteria, which we hope will flourish and maintain its own population. The function of probiotics is to provide healthy bacteria (the ones that normally reside in the gut) and promote healthy digestion of food, as well as to benefit the immune system. We all have probiotics and pathogenic bacteria in our intestinal tract and it is the balance between the two that help us to remain healthy. Probiotics can be of particular benefit to the animal with gastrointestinal and general immune system problems.

Because probiotics are live cultures, they are usually stable only if refrigerated. Some 'dry' versions are available and while many dogs benefit from them, I find that the refrigerated versions found at health food stores are best. You should know that not all probiotics are created equal. Some contain dairy and since some dogs have a hard time digesting dairy products, you are probably better off with a non-dairy version. Probiotics may also contain FOS, which is a sugar. This is not a bad thing because the culture feeds off the sugar and remains vital. However, some dogs do not handle FOS very well, just as they may not handle wheat or soy or any number of things.

I suggest that you look for as simple a product as possible. There has been discussion as to whether or not the various probiotics compete with each other at times. Offering a product that contains limited strains of probiotics seems to work best. Some dogs tolerate any type of probiotic while others are particularly sensitive to them. The only way to know what will work for *your* dog is to try small amounts and wait to see the reaction. Once you find the right brand, stick with it. Remember to check the expiration date before making your purchase, ensure the product was kept refrigerated in the store and keep it in your fridge at home as well. We must have tried at least ten different brands for Zoey. The one that works for her is Dophilus Plus from a company called Sisu.

Natural yogurt contains live cultures and is sometimes used for the same purpose as a powdered probiotic. This may be fine for your dog if he tolerates yogurt. However, keep in mind that you would have to feed buckets of yogurt to provide the number of organisms that are available in capsule form.

Probiotics are available in different strengths. As a rule, I look for a label that tells me there are four billion live organisms in a capsule. Knowing that the dose on the label is for humans, you would adjust the dose to suit the weight of your dog. So if an adult would take two capsules daily and the average adult weight is one hundred and fifty pounds, you know that this translates to one capsule for every seventy-five pounds of body weight. Therefore, your twenty-five pound dog would probably do well with one third of a capsule.

Once you find the probiotic that seems to agree with your dog, it may be wise to use it daily at first and then reduce to about 2-3 times per week. I've known many dogs that could not tolerate high doses of probiotics for an extended period of time. Always remember that a *balance* between various strains of bacteria needs to be maintained. We do not know what the gut of *your* dog contains at any given time and too much of a good thing can often cause a negative reaction.

Brewer's Yeast/Nutritional Yeast

These supplements are used primarily to provide a wide range of B vitamins. Most dogs enjoy the flavor that the yeast adds to foods, and in my experience, few have an adverse reaction to it. However, there *are* some dogs that cannot tolerate any form of yeast. The most common problems associated with this include redness or scratching which would indicate an allergy or sensitivity. I would not use yeast for dogs that have many allergies. Nor would I use it for dogs that tend toward yeast infections. Not because these yeasts would feed the yeast within a dog or be the cause of yeast infections. Yeast tends to overgrow in animals with a depressed immune system. When I see a dog with yeast problem, I am also seeing an animal that is likely to have food sensitivities so I choose not to add an ingredient that may exacerbate the problem.

When I do choose to use yeast as part of the diet, it is usually an addition of ¼ tsp to 1 cup of food and it is never used as the sole provider of B vitamins.

Bone Meal

Used to provide both calcium and phosphorus, bone meal has been given a bad rap. It is a cooked product, which means that some of the people feeding a raw diet are adamant about not using it. It is also said to be full of toxins such as lead. One theory suggests that if a cow had been raised on a farm situated near a highway, it would have inhaled toxic car fumes. Perhaps it was an *old* cow and so the bones would have had more years in which to absorb whatever toxins happened to be around. Heaven knows that there are any number of stories about what else might have happened to this theoretical cow.

Since stories abound, let's create another one! What if the cow was young, didn't live beside the highway and the bone meal that was produced from this animal had untraceable impurities when a lab did an analysis? It would still be a cooked product. However, if you can live with that, would this bone meal seem to be an option when you need to provide calcium and phosphorus?

When I began preparing food for Zoey, bone meal was one of the first supplements that I tried. Knowing how sensitive she is to every food and supplement and having read that bone meal was an evil addition to diets, my nerves were on edge. The last thing this girl needed was a 'toxic' substance. My findings surprised me. Lab analysis showed that the Swiss Herbal brand of bone meal has untraceable impurities. This is the brand that I carry and suggest to clients who do not have a high quality bone meal available to them. Look into bone meal for yourself. There are several brands on the market and all companies should be able to provide you with a laboratory assay.

Many European countries pulled bone meal off the shelves when Mad Cow Disease became a concern. Now *that* makes some sense. Fortunately, Canada has had only one case of Mad Cow Disease and that was from an animal that had been imported from the United Kingdom. Our laws prohibit the import of cattle and the country is reputed to be one of the safest places in the world for beef products in general.

Bone meal varies in its content of calcium and phosphorus. When you see a recipe that includes bone meal, it is important to know which brand of bone meal is being used. Substituting brands makes a world of difference to the final outcome of the calcium to phosphorus ratio.

Getting your own facts about bone meal is worth the effort. It is *not* the evil substance that some people claim it to be, but of course, you need to do some homework and find out about the purity of the product. Always be aware that bone meal made for human consumption is a totally different thing from garden bone meal. The garden variety *can* be toxic and should never be used for your pet. Blood and bone meal or meat and bone meal are vastly different from pure bone meal. Never substitute one for the other. My advice is to use only pure bone meal in the first place.

Egg Shells

One large eggshell contains about 2,000 mg of calcium and 80 mg of phosphorus. While temperatures and timing vary from oven to oven, most people wash and dry the shell before baking it in a 200-300 degree oven for 2-4 minutes. The cooled shell is then turned in- to a powder by putting it through a nut and seed grinder, or an herb mill, or small coffee bean grinder.

If salmonella concerns you, feeding raw eggshells would not be your choice, but many people do exactly this without worries.

Some dogs can eat chunks of eggshell without a problem but many others suffer from gastric upset. It may be that the sharp edges of broken shells irritate the intestines.

Di-Calcium Phosphate

Used to provide an addition of both calcium and phosphorus to the diet, di-calcium phosphate may be found at some pet stores. I came across it at a pharmacy although this is not the norm. As with bone meal, it seems that there can be some difference between the amounts of calcium and phosphorus available in each brand. You would not want to use di-calcium phosphate interchangeably with bone meal, just as you wouldn't substitute one brand of bone meal for another. When you find a recipe in a book that calls for a certain amount of bone meal, it would be worthwhile investigating how much calcium and phosphorus that bone meal was to provide, before substituting anything else.

Generic Calcium

When a dog is unable to handle various forms of calcium or when a diet calls for *only* a calcium addition, generic calcium can come to the rescue.

Calcium carbonate and calcium citrate keep the urine more neutral to basic in pH, while chloride and gluconate forms tend to help acidify the urine somewhat. The one to choose depends on what you want the urine to do. For most dogs, I lean toward using the carbonate or citrate forms.

Digestive Enzymes

Normally, the body is a wizard at manufacturing all the digestive enzymes necessary. Chronically ill pets can sometimes benefit from the addition of these enzymes in supplemental form. Your veterinarian is your best guide on this subject but I would like to share my personal experience and thoughts.

When a diet change is made, it is not unusual to see a looser stool, especially so when the new diet was introduced too quickly. A noisy digestive tract, gas, and sloppy stool are enough to send many pet guardians into panic mode. Commonly, the discussion of digestive enzymes comes up. Some people feel that with the addition of these enzymes, the dog will handle the diet switch more quickly and easily. This may or may not be true.

My goal in working with dogs is to see them thriving on their new diet. If the dog displays any of the symptoms listed above, I choose to take a step back and question what food might have been a problem for this animal and why this would be so. In other words, I am a firm believer that the *diet* needs to suit the dog. It is not the *dog* that needs to suit the diet!

Unless there is a history of this animal showing a need for digestive enzymes, I am in no hurry to use them. It makes more sense to me to consider that the dog might be having trouble with too much fat in the diet, or perhaps there is too much or too little fiber. The possibility of the diet being incorrect for *that* dog exists and should never be ignored or patched up with enzymes.

I question whether or not the addition of digestive enzymes might in fact be a problem at times. It may seem like a stretch to use the example of certain medications to make my point but consider this:

Some medications affect the 'normal' workings of body systems. For instance, prednisone is a drug that can cause steroid overdose, which over time causes the adrenals to stop making steroid. Please note that I am *not* comparing digestive enzymes to prednisone by any stretch of the imagination. However, when we introduce digestive enzymes into the body, it only makes sense that the body needs to produce fewer digestive enzymes of its own. In turn, the body may lose the ability to recognize the need to produce these enzymes as time goes on - just as prednisone and other drugs can 'confuse' the body into not producing normal amounts of a substance. Perhaps this is not a problem. Some people consider digestive enzymes to actually save the body from needing to work very hard at proper digestion. I believe that we are all meant to use the natural functions of our bodies and enzyme production is a naturally occurring event. Typically, when we give the body something that it already produces and doesn't need more of, it stops producing it.

My experience is that once a dog has been given digestive enzymes for a while, it is best to decrease the amount of enzymes slowly rather than do away with them overnight. The dogs that I've dealt with have been unable to digest food properly unless this weaning method was used. This points me to think that, indeed, the body had become somewhat reliant on an outside source of digestive enzymes and was sluggish when the need to produce them naturally arose.

That said, there are times when a dog seems to benefit from supplemental digestive enzymes. Chronic gastrointestinal problems and other medical conditions may leave a pet well suited for the addition of digestive enzymes. In these cases, I like to sprinkle the enzymes on the food, mix well and allow this mixture to sit for about ten minutes. This allows the enzymes to begin breaking down the food and I've found it to be especially useful for dogs that cannot tolerate fats very well.

Further discussion is sometimes requested when one of my clients begins to look at the array of digestive enzyme labels on the market. I often receive questions about which brand is best, what the heck some of these enzymes actually do and how to decide what a good quality product might be.

The brand name of the product is not important. Well known brand names do not assure us that a product is superior. A company can produce great quality items but may also carry a few inferior ones. What is more important is that the enzymes give us full spectrum activity, which means that the names of the enzymes themselves should look something like this:

Protease to break down protein
Lipase to break down fats
Amylase to break down carbohydrates
Cellulase to break down fiber
Lactase to break down milk products

There are two main varieties of digestive enzymes on the market. Some are plant-based enzymes, meaning that the enzymes are derived from plant-based sources. Others are 'regular' enzymes, which means that some of the enzymes (usually the protease) may be derived from an animal source. This is not usually a problem but unless you know the source of the protease, you could unknowingly be giving your dog something that s/he is allergic to.

There are more 'natural' enzymes derived from fruits, such as bromelain from pineapples. These do help digestion in some cases but I have also found that some dogs react quite strongly against them. *Your* dog may do very well on any form of digestive enzymes.

The point is simply to be aware that a dog can react to one form and not another.

When looking at labels, remember to read the fine print. Knowing that the product is free of yeast, soy, artificial colors and preservatives, corn and milk, is a good start because all of these items are usually considered to be common allergens.

Cod Liver Oil

This is the most commonly used fish liver oil in home-prepared diets and is thought to be beneficial. As with anything else, the claim needs to make some sense for the diet that *you* are feeding *your* dog. Cod liver oil adds fat (and therefore calories) to the diet as well as vitamins A and D and Omega 3 fatty acid.

The addition of fat to a diet that contains a high percentage of fat to begin with can lead to problems. Not only because weight gain can become an issue but also because many dogs can only tolerate so much fat in the diet. This is especially true for dogs that have weak pancreatic function.

Some people use cod liver oil to provide sufficient vitamin D in the diet. Since vitamin D is a crucial component in calcium absorption, it is easy to understand why we focus on it at times. But keep something in mind. One teaspoon of cod liver that contains 450 mg of vitamin D is sufficient (per day) for a dog that weighs about 37 kilograms or about 83 pounds. This same animal needs about 4,144 IU of vitamin A daily. The teaspoon of cod liver oil provides 4,500 IU of vitamin A. This 83 pound dog is receiving excess vitamin A but perhaps not so much that we would be really concerned. However, if this animal is also eating just a small amount of liver once per week, the vitamin A content of the diet soars to unacceptable levels.

Your dog also has the ability (just as humans do) to convert beta carotene from fruits and vegetables into vitamin A. It is the *preformed* version of vitamin A (from animal sources such as cod liver oil), which accumulates in the body and can become toxic at high levels.

Different brands of cod liver oil provide varying amounts of vitamins A and D. It is always wise to look at the label.

Essential Fatty Acids

The body cannot manufacture the essential fatty acids Omega 3 and Omega 6 from other elements. They must be supplied daily in the diet. Omega 3 and Omega 6 are two fatty acids that together:

- Form the membranes of every cell in the body
- Make up a large part of the structural and functional tissue in the brain
- Control the way cholesterol works
- Become prostaglandins, which play key roles in regulating the digestive, cardiovascular, immune and reproductive functions of the body
- Have vital roles in the functions of the brain, inflammation and healing, and body heat.

One of the first signs that a dog might display when the diet lacks essential fatty acids is poor skin and/or coat condition.

There has been much speculation and discussion as to what the ideal ratio of Omega 6 to Omega 3 might be. It is not unusual to hear people saying that the ratio should be 4:1 while others think that 10:1 is fine. The fact is that unless we calculate exactly how much of each of these essential fatty acids might be in a food to begin with, it is impossible to know how much supplementation is required. And even if we bothered to calculate everything precisely, we still don't know which ratio is ideal.

Taking nature as our guide, we might investigate what the ratios are in the natural diet of a wolf or wild dog. This may be an exercise in futility. Little is known and our pets may require different supplementation to address *personal* needs.

Most raw diets contain plenty of fat and depending on the foods you select, chances are that the Omega 6 predominates in the diet. Unless you happen to be feeding a lot of fish, which is a good source of Omega 3, you may want to add of Omega 3 in one form or another. Diets that include lean meats may require a form of Omega 6 and Omega 3, although there is no *established* requirement for Omega 3 in the canine diet to begin with. Still, I find it impossible to ignore what I see. Skin and coat seem to benefit greatly from the addition of Omega 3 even when there is no diagnosed disease. I've often used Wild Salmon oil as an addition to the diet of show dogs simply to enhance the coat quality.

Heat destroys essential fatty acids. It is important to remember to add oils to the food just before your dog is about to eat. To provide benefit, oils should be consumed in capsule form or cold pressed liquid. Liquid forms, however, become rancid quickly. Never give your dog rancid oil! If you live with a small dog and will not use the full bottle of oil before it spoils, gel capsules make much more sense. Gel capsules are also more convenient to use.

Zoey is highly sensitive to many oils. It took some time for me to discover that the best way to avoid a severe reaction (diarrhea with mucus and blood) was to continually rotate oils in her diet. By using a different oil in a four day rotation, Zoey maintains good skin and coat condition as well as her weight. We commonly use borage oil, flaxseed oil, wild salmon oil and primrose oil - each one on a different day.

Borage Oil

This oil provides high content of gamma-linolenic acid (GLA) and is usually well tolerated by dogs. I often use it in diets where the animal cannot handle much fat. Due to the high amount of GLA, the pet can receive what she or he seems to need without upsetting the digestive tract. Naturally, you would want to use a small amount and see if *your* dog is tolerant of this oil.

Evening Primrose Oil

Also known as Primrose Oil, this contains a high amount of GLA. It may relieve inflammation and pain and many women rely on it during their premenstrual cycle. I have found Primrose Oil to be of great benefit to dogs that suffer with allergies that affect the skin and create welts.

Safflower Oil

Cold pressed safflower oil has been a staple in the diets of many dogs that require an addition of Omega 6. If you choose to use safflower oil, ensure that the bottle is a dark color and does not allow light to enter. Once the bottle has been opened, and to prevent rancidity, try opening a gel cap of vitamin E and adding it to the bottle of oil. Give it a gentle shake and keep the oil refrigerated. The Omega 6 in safflower oil is pro-inflammatory which does not present a problem unless your dog has skin conditions such as allergies.

Canola Oil

Internet rumor says that canola oil is toxic. Nonsense! Canola oil provides Omega 6 and Omega 3 content although this oil, like safflower, is not appropriate for dogs that suffer with inflammatory conditions.

Corn Oil

A source of both Omega 6 and 3, this oil is probably the least expensive of all. Many dogs are allergic to corn however, and seem to react to this oil more than to others. As with safflower and canola oils, corn oil is not the best option for dogs with inflammatory conditions.

Flaxseed Oil

Rich in the n-3 polyunsaturated fatty acid alpha-linolenic acid, cold pressed flaxseed oil is commonly used in home-prepared diets. The addition of Omega 3 to the diet is very helpful for many conditions, including those that are linked to inflammation and for healthy skin and coat.

Some people prefer to use ground flaxseeds rather than the oil itself. This can work well for dogs that do not react negatively to the addition of extra fiber.

Wild Salmon Oil

Fish body oils are a good source of Omega 3. There are many fish body oils on the market. Do not confuse them with fish *liver* oils and never substitute one for the other. We already know that oils derived from liver are very high in preformed vitamin A and that this vitamin can be toxic to your pet if overfed.

Fish oils provide an activated form of Omega 3. I have had greater success when adding this to the diet rather than flaxseed oil, and I also seem to need less of it in order to note improvement of coat and skin condition.

Please notice that my oil of choice is *wild* salmon oil as opposed to regular salmon oil. Some people believe they are interchangeable but this is not so.

Consider that farm raised fish are provided with man made, artificial diets. These diets are, of course, limited to the nutrients that we know about and may not provide the array of nutrients in a natural diet. Nutrients may deteriorate quickly and as a result, the fish may in fact have nutritional deficiencies. In other words, processed fish food may offer the same benefits and limitations as processed dog food.

Furthermore, salmon is a carnivore. In the wild, this species thrashes wildly as it chases other fish for a natural meal. The omega 3 fatty acids in fish come from the phytoplankton in the food chain that fish eat. We see then, that this cannot be compared to an artificial diet and living conditions.

Since wild salmon live in our contaminated waters, we might think that the oil itself can harbor unacceptable levels of PCBs and other toxic substances. In fact, wild salmon contains far less of these hazards than the farmed variety. Mercury levels can be higher in wild salmon but the North Atlantic is the cleanest source known.

Lastly, but important to those of us who prefer to stay away from genetically modified foods, farmed salmon is being genetically modified.

Because Zoey reacts to almost everything, I made sure to test the wild salmon oil that I carry but you don't need to go that far. Companies should be able to provide you with a lab assay.

Apple Cider Vinegar

Touted as providing so many nutritional benefits that articles have been written about it, apple cider vinegar (ACV) is sometimes used in home-prepared diets. Proponents of ACV consider this supplement to benefit arthritis, gastric upsets and an entire host of other ailments as well as provide minerals. There seems to be divided opinion as to whether ACV acidifies the body or neutralizes acids or does anything at all since the body buffers itself so well.

People who feed a raw diet seem to be the most likely to include ACV in the food. Some claim that the addition helps the dog to digest bones. Others say that it helps the dog to digest fats. Still others tell me that it is the perfect solution to helping the dog digest meat. Most agree that it helps to reduce fat.

I have yet to see a report that impresses me regarding some of the claims but certainly, the reduction of fat can be true. There is no miracle here though. Take half a teaspoon of safflower oil and half a teaspoon of ACV and you will have cut down on the fat per teaspoon simply by the process of dilution.

If indeed ACV can be credited with the other claims, I still question why we need to add this to a diet that should be well suited to the dog to begin with. A dog that needs help in digesting food which is supposed to be good for him or her, might need a diet change rather than ACV.

Grapefruit Seed Extract

Grapefruit seed extract (GSE) has been touted as a broad spectrum antimicrobial with the ability to fight yeast, parasites and bacteria. It is sometimes used as an addition to raw diets or diluted with water and used as a soak for raw meat. The belief is that harmful bacteria will be killed but this extract does not affect many of the very bacteria that some people worry about. For instance, it does not address salmonella. Furthermore, grapefruit seed extract may be preserved and it is this *preservative* that may in fact be the item that offers 'protection' against certain bacteria.

You should know that grapefruit seed extract has a very bitter taste. Use just a few drops more than what your dog can tolerate and you're likely to notice him vomiting or turning away from his food. I have used GSE as just 2-3 drops in water when Zoey was fighting off a yeast infection. It seemed to help but I would not use it in her food and not on a daily basis.

Multi vitamin/mineral Complex

Many home-prepared diets lack some vital vitamins and minerals. Usually, it's the mineral deficiency that needs to be addressed although in some cases, the whole diet needs a quick fix. Commonly, we think that if we feed a great variety of foods, we have covered all the basic nutritional needs of an animal. But let's take a closer look.

Sometimes we choose nice ingredients but they're not nutrient dense. For instance, spinach provides iron but not much per gram. The amount that would have to be fed is far more than any dog could eat to meet requirements. I can almost hear you saying that few people would look to spinach as the main ingredient in a dog's diet and iron might come from liver instead. Say you have a 50 pound dog and you feed 100gr of raw chicken liver. You are providing about 8.5 mg of iron when this dog needs a minimum of 14.77 mg of iron daily. However, you are also providing 2,549 IU of vitamin A when this animal needs a minimum of 1,650 IU daily. If you were to feed 200gr of chicken liver daily, the iron requirement is met but now the amount of vitamin A being provided is well above what it should be. Remember that vitamin A is stored in the body and can be toxic when high levels are fed.

This is only one example of situations where a simple multi vitamin/mineral tablet makes life easier. That said, some home-prepared diets *can* meet the needs of an animal just as we do with humans. I consider a multi vitamin/mineral tablet to be an insurance policy when the diet falls short of where we believe it should be.

A special situation arises when we live with dogs that are highly sensitive to a variety of foods. In these cases, we may have to feed a restricted diet without much variety. For these animals, a multi vitamin/mineral tablet can literally save the dog from a life of misery and ill health.

To date, I have not found a multi vitamin/mineral tablet that I can say works for all dogs. Of the ones that I'm aware of, Canine Basic Nutrients by Thorne Research seems to be one of the best. The problem I continue to run into is that vitamins for pets include flavoring agents, which many dogs do not tolerate. Fillers, binders and other additives seem to cause gastric upset for some animals while others begin to scratch, usually indicating an intolerance. We can use high quality human grade supplements, but this introduces another problem because the formulation usually includes dosages that are inappropriate for the size of our pets. Some children's vitamins can work although here again, we run into the problem of sugar and flavoring agents being included most of the time.

Chapter 13
INDIVIDUALLY APPROPRIATE DIETS

What most of us really want is a simple way of feeding our dogs without having to worry about nutrient deficiencies and excesses. After all, this is one of the reasons that pet foods are so popular.

In a noble effort to emulate Mother Nature and rid ourselves of concerns over nutrient values, some of us feed a diet that includes a great deal of variety and trust that this will balance out over time. Indeed this can happen but unfortunately, not all dogs can handle a great variety of foods. Some dogs have allergies while others deal with medical conditions that simply do not respond well to a variety of feeding methods. The *diet* may very well be biologically appropriate but perhaps the *dog* is not! We must address the needs of the individual rather than the species.

Zoey used to eat nothing but cooked turkey (25%) and acorn squash (75%). This would make any veterinary nutritionist cringe. Raw feeders usually laughed in disbelief. Yet the diet was very real and the only thing that kept Zoey's raging colitis under control. I use one of my own dogs as an example so that you can see just how ill suited a dog can be to what others might claim is a perfect diet.

If there is one point that I hope you will consider, it is that *your* dog is unique. He or she will never be just a genetic model. Your pet is unlikely to do well on a set diet plan unless you observe and react to individual needs.

How do you know what the needs are? Providing that your veterinarian agrees that you have a healthy pet, put the diet books down long enough to really watch your dog.

If you see a high-energy animal, the diet may require more fat to support energy needs. If the dog cannot tolerate this (as evidenced by vomiting or a sloppy stool), you might choose to feed a higher carbohydrate diet to support the energy needs.

The dog with runny eyes and/or itchy body parts is very likely to be dealing with allergies. These could be environmental in nature but could just as easily be related to diet. Some dogs have food allergies while others may have nutrition-responsive skin disorders. In this case you might try feeding a diet that contains very limited ingredients. Chances are that your pet is allergic to the meat source in the diet so using a novel protein (one which the pet has never consumed before) would be a good start. Combine this with a grain such as rice, which contains no gluten, because some dogs have an allergic response to gluten. You might choose to use a vegetable instead. Feed only these two ingredients to an otherwise healthy animal, for at least four weeks and preferably, six to eight weeks. You would want to add a calcium source and possibly a multi vitamin/mineral providing it was considered hypo-allergenic. If the dog seems to have improved, challenge him or her by using a different protein. Should the original symptoms return, go back to the original protein that seemed to agree with the pet. If symptoms do not improve, you might try a different protein, vegetable or grain. The great majority of allergies are to a meat or grain source.

Rules of Thumb

Unless your dog happens to have an allergic response to a vegetable, there is a basic rule of thumb. Above ground vegetables tend to loosen stool while root vegetables tend to firm up the stool.

Root vegetables tend to be sweeter in taste and most dogs enjoy them. Green leafy vegetables are not always as well accepted but since they offer valuable nutrients, they should be provided in the diet. Combining both root vegetables and green leafy varieties usually works to provide the correct balance of fiber to avoid messy or hard stool.

Knowing that minerals interact, we want to provide a variety of vegetables rather than sticking with one or two. Having said this, it is also a good idea not to use every vegetable in the book within each meal. By providing 2-4 different vegetables on a daily basis, we are at less risk of repeating the same mineral interactions

Vegetables and grains contain phytates. Phytates bind calcium, making the mineral less available to your pet. For this reason, feeding vegetables and grains away from raw meaty bones makes sense. If you choose to feed a cooked diet in the form of a stew, you might want to consider using enough calcium to meet 1.25-1.5 times the amount of calcium noted by the NRC. This attempts to compensate for the binding of calcium.

Dogs do not have the ability to break down the cellulose walls of vegetables and fruits. If you feed your dog a raw carrot, you will see pieces of undigested carrot in the stool. Feeding vegetables and fruits is best when these items are properly prepared. Cooking destroys the cellulose walls, as does mechanically crushing a raw vegetable. This is easily achieved by running the vegetable through a juicer. You can feed the pulp alone or include the juice. I prefer to use an electric meat grinder. You may opt to put cooked vegetables through a food processor but the final outcome must be a food that is pulverized. Feed raw or cooked vegetables in any other way and you will notice pieces of undigested matter in the stool; proof that your pet is not digesting this well. However, some vegetables such as raw carrots can work well to clean teeth and provide enjoyable chewing time for your dog. When used for these purposes, I'm not as concerned about digestibility.

Remember to use protein. Many people feed a raw diet that is chock full of raw meaty bones and very small amounts of foods that contain enough protein. These diets provide a lot of fat, which in turn can lead to obesity. In many cases however, the dog is genuinely hungry because s/he is lacking in vital protein and craves more food to meet natural need. If you choose to use the wild role model as your example, consider that a rabbit or deer has quite a bit of meat on those bones!

Bones tend to firm up the stool. Use too many raw, meaty bones and your dog can end up having a blockage. Remember that moderation in all things is usually best.

Poor skin and coat conditions usually respond well to an addition of Omega 3 from fish body oils or flaxseed oil. Nevertheless, there could be other factors in the diet that might need to be addressed. Zinc and B vitamins, for example, also affect the skin.

Diets

A book on canine diet is expected to include at least a few recipes. I must admit that this has been the most difficult part of this book for me. I am *not* a believer in generic diets. There are a number of books already on the market that provide a variety of recipes that have worked for some dogs and been a disaster for others. Again, I will stress the fact that your dog deserves better than a generic diet plan.

Nevertheless, I believe that it may be important to show a few examples of diets and discuss the shortcomings that may not be noticed at first glance but could exist. It is my hope that you will be able to use some of these diets but also, that you will see why a multi vitamin/mineral or another food addition is a good insurance policy. All of these diets are geared towards a generally healthy, normal dog. *Note:* Before starting any new diet for a dog with health concerns, it is wise to consult your veterinarian.

Please note that the bone meal in these recipes is by Swiss Herbal, and contains 660 mg of calcium and 280 mg of phosphorus per teaspoon. If you use another brand of bone meal, adjustments will be required. Simply compare the amount of calcium and phosphorus in your chosen brand of bone meal to the amounts noted above.

Also note that caloric intake needs to be managed per individual. While I have suggested the weight that a given recipe should support, this can vary quite dramatically and you would want to feed the appropriate amount for *your* dog.

Meats may be ground or cut into suitably sized pieces. Vegetables should be minced, steamed or cooked thoroughly. The amounts noted in these diets are daily rations unless noted otherwise.

Raw Beef, RawVegetables, Bone Meal

A dog that tolerates raw foods but cannot handle raw meaty bones, may do well on this beef diet:

4 oz beef chuck, ¼" fat, raw
2 oz beef heart, raw
3 oz romaine lettuce, raw
4.5 oz sweet potato, raw
¼ tsp safflower oil
500 IU wild salmon oil
1 1/8 tsp bone meal powder
100 IU vitamin E
12.5 mg multi B vitamin, 3-4 weekly

This should support the weight of a 10 pound dog. It provides 36% Kcal from protein, 35% Kcal from carbohydrates and 29% Kcal from fat.

Cooked Turkey With Grain, Vegetable and Bone Meal

This is a fairly low antigen diet. As a result of using only turkey, it is low in copper, zinc and just borderline in iron. Nevertheless, it is indicative of what many people must feed when the dog tolerates only one protein source, and cannot handle much in the way of fiber from grains. The amount of squash used here may seem high but I've had great luck with this type of diet for fiber responsive conditions. This diet uses a multi vitamin to address the deficiencies noted above. You may want to note that adding kelp and/or alfalfa in any reasonable amount would *not* alter the deficiencies of this diet and could further upset a sensitive digestive tract.

3.5 oz dark turkey meat, roasted
½ cup white rice, boiled
2 cups acorn squash, boiled
½ tsp turkey fat
¾ tsp safflower oil
1 ¾ tsp bone meal powder

½ tsp flaxseed oil
200 IU vitamin E
multi vitamin/mineral

This should support the weight of a 16-17 pound dog. It provides 27% Kcal from protein, 51% Kcal from carbohydrates and 22% Kcal from fat.

Last Minute Dinner

Despite loving my dogs, I admit to forgetting to thaw some food for them once in a while. If this hasn't already happened to you, it's bound to sooner or later. The following diet uses up that smidge of leftover liver in the fridge. It is not a 'balanced' diet but is fine to use the odd time. Should you want to feed it more often though, a multi vitamin/mineral tablet is in order!

5gr beef liver, braised
4 large, whole eggs, poached
125gr brown rice, raw
50gr spinach, boiled, no salt
½ tsp canola oil
4 tsp bone meal powder
pinch of iodized table salt
200 IU vitamin E

This should feed a 30 pound dog. The iodized salt addresses the need for chloride as well as providing iodine, but elevates the sodium content. This is a low protein diet with only 19% Kcal from protein, 51% Kcal from carbohydrates and 30% Kcal from fat.

Chicken Necks, Raw Meat with Cooked and Raw Vegetable

For better or worse, many raw feeders use chicken as the predominant meat source in the diet. It is not uncommon to note changes in the color of the coat and some skin problems cropping up several months to one year after this sort of diet is fed. We'll see why this may be the case in the following example.

Note that I have included cooked potato in this diet. While some people claim that potatoes are problematic for all dogs, I have yet to see this unless the pet cannot tolerate potato in the first place. This diet is an example of combining both cooked and raw foods, which is sometimes what a dog needs in order to have a good stool. If you choose to use something other than potato, make sure that you look at the nutrient profile of your selected food.

3 oz skinless chicken necks, raw
2.5 oz chicken light meat with skin, raw
2.5 oz chicken dark meat, no skin, raw
1/8 chicken liver, raw
4.5 oz potato, boiled, no salt, cooked in skin
2 oz broccoli, raw
500 IU salmon oil
200 IU vitamin E
multi vitamin/mineral

This should support the weight of a 17 pound dog. It provides 39% Kcal from protein, 24% Kcal from carbohydrates and 37% Kcal from fat. This is a high-energy diet suited for active dogs.

People who use more chicken necks and less meat will be providing more fat and this diet is already fairly high in fat content. However, the bigger problem is that despite being a good source of other nutrients, this is low in copper, iron and zinc. Chicken is naturally low in these nutrients. Feeding more liver would address part of this problem but not enough of it, and the vitamin A level would soar to unacceptable levels. Feeding more necks would provide more zinc - on paper. Remember that calcium binds zinc and we do not know how much of the zinc in bones is actually available to your dog.

Feeding a diet that offers limited ingredients also means that we are feeding limited quantities of vital nutrients. It is crucial that you feed more than chicken as a meat source but reality can be different.

I knew that I *should* feed Zoey something other than turkey and squash but she simply didn't tolerate other foods. If you are in this predicament, you must use a multi vitamin/mineral tablet to compensate for the deficiencies.

Balance Over Time
A Raw Diet Plan That Includes a Bit of Grain

Since we know that balancing nutrients over time is a natural event, many people choose to feed a diet that consists of several food items. This makes good sense if your dog tolerates variety. The following is an example of what foods and quantities you might feed to help accomplish this over a *one-week* period.

½ oz beef liver and/or 1 oz chicken giblets*, raw
2 medium, whole fresh eggs, raw
7 oz beef chuck, ¼" fat, raw
2 oz beef heart, raw
7 oz turkey, light meat with skin, raw
2 oz Atlantic sardines, canned in oil
16 oz skinless chicken necks
6 oz skinless turkey necks

24 oz sweet potato, raw
10.5 oz turnip, raw
3.5 oz broccoli, raw
3.5 oz celery, raw
2 inner leaves, romaine lettuce, raw
2 oz spinach, raw
½ cup brown rice, boiled
500 mg Wild Salmon Oil per day
150 IU Vitamin E per day

This should support the weight of a 14 pound dog and provides 36% Kcal of protein, 32% Kcal of carbohydrates and 32% Kcal of fat.

*Feeding *both* liver and giblets for a full week drives the vitamin A content of this diet to approximately double the requirement.

Since not all foods provide sufficient B vitamins and these vitamins are water soluble, I would opt to include 12.5 mg of a multi B vitamin 3-4 times per week.

Turkey and Vegetable, Raw Diet Without Grain

1.3 oz (38gr) skinless turkey neck
4 oz turkey, dark meat with skin, raw
7 oz butternut squash, raw
2 oz spinach, raw
1,000 IU Wild Salmon Oil
Multi B vitamin (12.5 mg)
100 IU vitamin E

This simple diet provides 43% Kcal of protein, 33% Kcal of carbohydrates and 24% Kcal of fat. It should support the weight of a

9-11 pound dog. Being relatively high in protein, this kind of plan is best suited to the very energetic/athletic dog.

Please note that I have included a multi B vitamin. You may choose to use liver or another meat source that would provide a range of Bs but be careful not to overdo the vitamin A content in this case.

Raw and Cooked, A Seafood Meal

If you have some canned clams left over, here's a good way to use them up. Note that the sodium content of this recipe is high (about 4 times the norm). You can reduce the amount of clams and increase the amount of cod in order to reduce sodium but remember that this alters the rest of the nutrient profile dramatically. Sodium isn't a big problem unless heart failure, hypertension or other cardiovascular or metabolic disorder make it a contraindication.

80gr (2.8 oz) skinless turkey neck
3 oz cooked cod
2 oz canned clams, drained
7 oz sweet potato, raw
1 oz asparagus, raw
2 tsp safflower oil
200 IU vitamin E

This should support the weight of a 19-20 pound dog and provides 38% Kcal of protein, 38% Kcal of carbohydrates and 24% Kcal of fat.

Chicken Back, Raw diet without grain

1 ½ oz chicken back with skin, raw
1 oz lamb shoulder, blade, 1/8" fat, raw

2 oz beef heart, raw
5 oz turnip, raw
1 small celery stalk (5"), raw
1 oz carrot, raw
500 IU wild salmon oil

This should support the weight of 7-8 pound dog and provides 34% Kcal from protein, 24% Kcal from carbohydrates and 42% Kcal from fat.

Chicken Wings, Raw Diet Without Grain

3 ½ oz chicken wings, raw
2 oz beef chuck, ¼" fat, raw
1 oz chicken giblets, raw
6 oz butternut squash, raw
4 oz yam, raw
¼ cup spinach, raw
500 IU wild salmon oil
¼ tsp alfalfa powder
200 IU vitamin E
multi vitamin/mineral

This should support the weight of a 19 pound dog. It provides 25% Kcal from protein, 36% Kcal from carbohydrates and 40% Kcal from fat. The multi vitamin/mineral has been added to compensate for the low level of copper in this diet. The copper provided here is slightly below requirement per the current NRC guidelines. Feeding these combinations of foods in conjunction with other, more 'complete' diets listed, may provide sufficient copper but a multi vitamin/mineral complex acts as an insurance policy if you have any doubts.

Lamb, Cooked Diet Without Grain

4 oz lamb shoulder, blade, ¼" fat, braised
1 cup sweet potato, boiled, no salt, mashed
½ cup spinach, boiled, no salt, drained
¼ cup turnip, boiled, no salt, drained, mashed
500 IU wild salmon oil
2 ¼ tsp bone meal
200-250 IU vitamin E

This should support the weight of a 25 pound dog and provides 25% Kcal from protein, 48% Kcal from carbohydrates and 27% Kcal from fat.

Rabbit, Raw Diet Without Grain

120 gr. (4.22 oz) rabbit with bone, raw
12 oz acorn squash, raw
2 oz watercress, raw
10 oz. turnip, raw
2 medium, whole eggs, raw
100-150 IU vitamin E

This should support the weight of a 14-15 pound dog and provides 30% Kcal from protein, 42% Kcal from carbohydrates and 28% Kcal from fat.

Cooking a Raw Diet

Once we do this, it is obviously no longer a raw diet. However, using the recipe from a raw diet and cooking it can work. I've done this myself from time to time. All raw meaty bones need to be finely ground in this case. I've been known to grind them twice if I feel any bone shards and simply simmer the mixture for a couple of minutes. This was how I began to wean Zoey to raw meaty bones when she couldn't tolerate raw foods. It is a nice way to provide calcium and phosphorus in the correct ratio and I still do this sometimes.

The nutrient composition of the diet changes somewhat, of course, but the amount of calcium and phosphorus remain stable. A friend of mine feeds her dogs this way and had the diet analyzed at a lab. It worked out very well. Just keep in mind that some nutrients are heat sensitive and you might want to seriously consider using a multi vitamin/mineral complex to compensate for this.

Ensure that you add water or broth when you feed cooked, ground, meaty bones. As they cook, moisture evaporates. You end up feeding a mass of ground bone, which can cause fecal impaction. Simply add enough water to make this a moist meal. A good amount of vegetables and healthy oils also help to keep the bowels moving.

Introducing a New Diet

Some people go 'cold-turkey' meaning that they switch from pet food to real food in one quick move. Some dogs tolerate this but the great majority don't and will react by having messy stool at the very least. In my opinion, a slow introduction is always best and rarely upsets the digestive tract. If you choose to feed a cooked diet, simply increasing the portion of real food while decreasing the portion of processed food over a period of about five days seems to work well.

For those who want to feed raw, meaty bones, introducing these slowly is advisable. Many dogs require some time to adjust to the fat in this food. Perhaps the easiest way to switch to a raw diet that includes bones, is to combine all foods into a mixture (grinding the raw meaty bones is a good option in this instance) and feeding small amounts of this mix while beginning to decrease the processed food.

How Much to Feed

People feeding their own home-prepared diets rather than following recipes, often wonder how much they should be feeding. The simple answer is to feed the amount that is required for your dog to maintain optimum body weight. There is no hard and fast rule for the total amount of food to feed because each animal differs from the next. The couch potato may require far fewer calories than his on-the-go brother. Metabolism varies as well.   Different foods offer varying numbers of calories. It doesn't take long to discover how much to feed and I tell people not to be overly concerned. Manage your dogs' weight by keeping a hand on the ribs and an eye on the bathroom scale.

Ideally, your dog will have a thin and firm covering of flesh over the rib cage. The ribs should not be visible but you should be able to feel them easily if you run your hands over the area gently. This is a common way of determining proper weight but some dogs are like people - they can be pear shaped. In other words, they may carry more weight in the rump area. Use the scale to determine weight gain or loss rather than just feeling the rib cage. You veterinarian is a great guide and asking for his/her opinion about the ideal weight of your dog is a good starting point.

Theory vs. Reality

A diet plan can be perfect on paper and totally useless in reality. That's because each dog is unique. We can calculate calories and the correct ratios of foods to support the calorie intake but what if the dog doesn't eat all the food we think she should? What happens when your dog eats only three-quarters of the supposedly correct amount to support his body weight and in reality, is perfectly capable of maintaining his weight this way. In this case, all plans are out the window! The same is true for processed dog food. Calculations can fall short when the animal isn't able to consume enough food to support the body's requirements for nutrients.

A multi vitamin/mineral tablet or capsule should be seriously considered. The other approach is to search for food items that are naturally higher in nutrients. Beef, for example, is a good source of copper. You might choose to feed this more often and therefore supply enough of this mineral. Despite the fact that your dog is eating less, he is likely to obtain the nutrients he needs if the food choices are very rich in each nutrient. In other words, you want to ensure that food choices are nutrient dense.

Feeding your dog a variety of foods will help to address some deficiencies but is not a guarantee that all needs will be met. This is especially the case when the dog is not eating *enough* of each food. Again, a multi vitamin/mineral tablet or capsule can be a big help in these situations.

Summary

- Runny eyes and itchy body parts may suggest an allergic reaction.

- Some dogs are allergic to gluten rather than grains per se.

- Observing your own dog closely can make the difference between really understanding his needs and attempting to accommodate them by guessing.

- Above ground vegetables tend to loosen stool. Root vegetables tend to firm the stool.

- Feeding vegetables and/or grains away from raw meaty bones may allow better absorption of calcium.

- All vegetables must be fed in a manner that allows their cellulose walls to be destroyed as much as possible. Mechanical breakdown or cooking can accomplish this.

- A diet that provides sufficient calories to maintain weight may nevertheless leave the dog genuinely hungry.

- Bones tend to firm the stool.

- Multi vitamin/mineral formulas may be required when the dog is unable to eat a variety of foods or sufficient amounts of these foods to provide proper nutrients.

- Introducing a new diet slowly is likely to result in fewer gastric upsets.

Chapter 14
POOP PATROL

What goes in must come out and some of us are avid poop watchers. This is especially the case when a new diet is introduced because we look for miracles. If the dog had chronic diarrhea in the past, we want that perfect tootsie roll stool now to ensure that we're on the right track. If we've read books that promise a certain diet will produce very firm, small stool, we want to see it right away. It's an exciting time for dog enthusiasts albeit a little embarrassing if the neighbor catches you doing a high five after poop inspection!

What does the perfect stool look like? When should we be concerned? Are small, hard, dry stools something to celebrate?

We all know a healthy stool when we see one. It isn't shiny, has no mucus covering and doesn't include blood. Black stool can be indicative of bleeding in the upper area of the intestinal tract. Fresh, red blood can indicate a problem in the lower bowel. Like people, dogs can vary in their stool production and 'normal' isn't necessarily the same for all individuals. However, mucus and blood are never good signs. Mucus can be due to parasites or inflammation. It is often considered to be 'detox' by those who believe that this is normal. In fact, mucus in the stool should be a very infrequent occurrence. It indicates a problem and very often, there has been an irritation in the digestive tract that needs to be addressed.

Some people celebrate a hard, small stool but let's be reasonable about this. Passing boulders is uncomfortable and often painful. Rock hard stools are *not* normal. Wolves gorge when they capture prey and then have diarrhea. Sometimes, people feed a raw diet while looking at the wild role models but then expect and celebrate small, rock hard stool. This makes little sense and can be a problem. We may want to believe that small amounts of feces is due to the fact that the dog has absorbed the food so well that little is left to excrete. This may be true in part but the flip side is that the bowel may be impacting with stool, because the dog isn't able to pass it. Healthy dogs might strain a little during defecation but not for a very long time.

Many dogs will kick their back feet and walk away from the feces. They do not remain in a hunched position while walking away. This arched position is sometimes associated with pain.

Stool color often depends on the diet. For instance, feeding quite a bit of liver can make the stool look very dark. Feeding orange vegetables such as squash can tint the stool to an orange hue. Kaleidoscope colored stool is not abnormal although it should not be colored due to visible pieces of undigested foods. A bit of this is acceptable but if you see chunks of undigested matter along with other signs such as straining during defection or mucus in the stool, it may be time to chat with your veterinarian.

Some people feeding a raw diet that includes bones appreciate seeing a white stool. That is, the stool turns white as it dries and sometimes is white even during defecation. In some circles, this is celebrated as a sign that excess calcium is being excreted and translated to mean that sufficient calcium has been absorbed. In fact, some of these stools are very dry and make clean up a breeze for the owner but the dog may not be as quick to celebrate. It is not difficult to provide sufficient calcium and the tables showing the nutrient values of raw, meaty bones, show this clearly. I see no point in providing so much that the stool becomes hard, dry and painful to excrete. Some veterinarians are concerned about what this constant abrasion might be doing in the long run. A stool that turns white in the sun is fine as long as the dog is not laboring too long to do what nature intended. The goal is to have a healthy happy dog - not a rock hard stool.

Some people wonder how long it takes for real food to pass through the system. A few books and many people suggest that raw food passes through the stomach in five hours while processed food takes ten to fifteen hours. This is not quite accurate. Processed foods can take as little as five hours. The following provides interesting information by Dr. DC Twedt, DVM DACVIM, a respected gastroenterologist who states that the average emptying time is usually 5-8 hours and anything over 10 hours is considered delayed.[11] The mention of 15 hours appears and some people use this time frame to state that the transit time of processed food is 15 hours. This is not so.

"Vomiting of a meal greater than 10 hours following eating is suggestive of a gastric retention disorder. Barium mixed with food appears to be a better test of gastric emptying of solids and may help document disorders of motility. Studies in control dogs found barium sulfate suspension mixed with ground kibble took from 5 to 15 hours to leave the stomach with the majority of the animals emptying in approximately 8 to 10 hours. Animals with markedly prolonged emptying time following a barium meal are usually clinical for gastric motility disorders".

---

[11] David Twedt, DVM, DACVIM, 1999, Diplomat, American College of Veterinary Internal Medicine, Professor, Dept. of Clinical Sciences, Colorado Sate University College of Veterinary Medicine and Biomedical Sciences, Fort Collins, Colorado

Bones In The Stool

I've stopped counting how many emails I receive about pieces of bones found in the stool. The stool of wild canids sometimes has bones in it. Often, these bones are wrapped in some of the hair of the prey. This hair is presumed to act as a barrier against the rough parts of jagged bone. Dogs that eat whole bones may be able to pass pieces of bone without a problem but nobody agrees whether or not this creates a problem in the long run. Will the possible scraping of the bowel cause injury or weakness down the road? Is it instead quite normal and nothing to worry about? I can't say, and neither can anyone else, because some dogs seem to have problems from these undigested pieces of bone while others do not.

If you are uncomfortable with the idea of bones showing up in the stool or your dog has a gastro problem to begin with, grinding is a good option. Not only because it removes the worries but if you are wondering about calcium absorption, grinding appears to have benefits.

Logic says that a wider surface area would make a nutrient more available. In other words, a hunk of bone will only be digested to a point, with some dogs being able to do a better job of it than others. Spread this bone out into a flatter surface by grinding it and the availability of nutrients should be improved. Here is an interesting study to consider. It relates to the increased surface area as well as the thickness of a bone.[12]

---

[12] The Rate of Calcium Extraction From Chicken Bone: David Frerichs, Anna Marie Lipski, Alice Wu, Christopher Hack – University of Pennsylvania, 2000

"The rate of calcium extraction from three chicken femurs was determined by varying surface areas of a whole bone filled with wax, a longitudinally halved bone, and a ground bone. Each bone was suspended in a beaker that was filled with 900mL of 1M HCl solution. Samples were taken from the beakers for a period of 4.5 hours at 15 minute intervals and then twice daily for four days afterwards. The samples were then analyzed by atomic absorption spectrophotometry. The results showed that the ground bone released the most calcium, 69.92% the estimated maximum calcium available, as opposed to 61.24% for the halved bone and 52.14% for the whole bone. Experimental data also revealed that the original hypothesis of the experiment was false - surface area was not the only determining factor in the rate of calcium extraction from a chicken femur. The halved bone had 10% greater surface area than the whole bone, but a calcium extraction rate that was 290% greater."

It would seem that both surface area and thickness of bone makes a dramatic impact to the availability of calcium. Actual extraction of this mineral is likely to differ when we compare lab work to that of the gastric tracts of dogs. Still, it seems reasonable that this study would have some meaning and that we might expect greater absorption from ground bones than from whole bones.

Summary

- Stool should be firm without being so hard and small that the dog is uncomfortable during defecation.

- Stool color depends on the diet. It is not uncommon to notice very dark stool after a meal that included liver.

- Red blood in the stool is not normal. A black, tarry stool is not normal.

- Mucus can indicate parasites or inflammation and should not be ignored.

- Diarrhea can quickly dehydrate a dog. Ensuring the pet drinks well while holding a 12-24 hour fast (for a healthy dog) should help to rectify the problem. If the pet is still unwell, a veterinarian should be consulted sooner rather than later.

- Some people consider undigested pieces of bone in the stool to be normal. Others feel this is a hazard. If in doubt, grind.

- Processed foods can take as little as five hours to pass through the stomach - the same claim that is made for raw foods. Gastric motility disorders seem to be the cause for slow digestion rather than the food itself.

- The availability of calcium from bones may be affected by the thickness of the bone itself and by grinding.

Chapter 15
NOW WHAT?

Much of the mail I receive is from people who started feeding a home-prepared diet and saw great results only to encounter problems down the road. The most common problems are cited here. I hope that you will find a few answers that are helpful. Keep in mind that some of the things mentioned here can be related to more serious health issues. A dietary concern should only be considered once a veterinarian has ruled out the possibility of disease factors.

The coat was shiny but now it's dull

I've seen this happen with diets that are too lean or when either Omega 3 or 6 fatty acids are too predominant. There is also the chance that your dog would benefit from *other* oils rather than the ones you are currently using. For instance, I've had greater success with wild salmon oil than with flaxseed oil and a rotation of oils can be very helpful to some dogs. When the diet is too lean, I'm very partial to the inclusion of borage and primrose oils as well.

He was eating well but now refuses the food

If this problem is not combined with illness, it's possible that your dog is simply feeling satisfied and does not require the amount of food you think he should have. Some dogs go on a voluntary fast for a day without there being a problem. If this is not the case, you might have a finicky eater. Hungry dogs eat heartily, but there may be more to the story.

Some dogs have incredible intuitive instinct and will refuse foods that upset their bodies. If you have just added a new ingredient to the diet, this could be the reason that your dog doesn't want to eat. He may be suspicious of the new smell or something in this mix isn't sitting well with him in the first place. If he acts hungry but refuses the food you offer, I would not automatically assume that he is acting like a spoiled brat. Sometimes dogs really *do* know best!

However you do not want to fall into the trap of offering one food after another to see which one the dog chooses. This can certainly create a picky eater. Ignoring the request for food for an hour or more and offering a new food at that time would maintain your position as pack leader. But give the dog a chance to eat something that might agree with him.

She's always asking for more food

While it's possible that this is happening because your dog loves the new diet, it is just as possible that she is genuinely hungry.

You might maintain your weight by eating a chocolate bar or two a day simply due to the calorie content of these treats. You will feel true hunger during the day though. The same is true when a dog is fed a diet that is high in fat because we need to feed little of it in order to maintain body weight. As a matter of fact, there are hungry dogs that are overweight and people sometimes think they have a piglet on their hands. While this *can* be true it is not always the case. The dog simply doesn't feel full enough.

Look at the diet and see if you can cut back on fat. Replacing those calories with some high fiber foods such as vegetables and/or grains while possibly increasing the protein content (if the diet is low in protein), can translate to a happier dog that does not beg for food all day long.

The nails are brittle

I find this to be one of the first signs of a problem with calcium absorption. Looking at the diet more closely can be helpful. Not only do you want to ensure that calcium supply is sufficient but the calcium to phosphorus ratio needs to be correct as well. Is your dog receiving enough vitamin D? A bit more time in direct sunlight would probably take care of the vitamin D problem, if it exists. Is there enough magnesium in the diet?

If you know that all of the above are fine, look at the rest of the diet. Something as simple as a vitamin B complex tablet can be helpful. Remember that nutrients interact and not all diets provide enough of each nutrient *when it is needed*. Also remember that *your* dog is not likely to be the textbook version of the average dog. But it is the average dog that diet formulations are based on. This means that you need to consider absorption of nutrients rather than looking only at numbers. Since you cannot know exactly what the dog is absorbing, it is a good idea to look at various options. For example, if you have been using di-calcium phosphate as the calcium/phosphorus source, you might switch to bone meal or raw, meaty bones.

My dog is not drinking very much

This is usually noticed after the first few days of feeding a home-prepared-diet. Kibble is a dry food that lacks moisture and your dog is likely to have been drinking more if that's what he was previously eating. Since fresh food diets provide quite a bit of natural moisture, and are not high in sodium content, most dogs need to drink less. You can add a bit of water to the meals if you're really concerned. If you want to encourage your dog to drink more, offering broth can be helpful. I sometimes use a homemade chicken broth that has been de-fatted.

Chicken Broth

4-5 cups of good quality water
2 chicken wings
1 celery stalk
1 small carrot
a few sprigs of parsley
½ small potato

Simmer all ingredients until meat is soft. Remove all foods from broth. Let cool. Place in refrigerator overnight or until fat solidifies. Skim layer of fat and discard. Divide into servings and freeze for use as needed.

This broth has helped many dogs through a needed fasting period when they had an upset stomach. In these cases, I add just a pinch of salt to provide some iodine, chloride and sodium. My own dogs consider this to be a huge treat. In the summer I freeze it in an ice cube tray so I can give each of them a cube to enjoy outdoors. During the colder months, I warm the broth up on the stove for a minute and they whine in anticipation.

Discharges

When dogs begin to have excess tearing, noses that drip or ear discharges, an allergy may be the problem. Whether or not this is due to environmental or dietary factors is something you can attempt to discover by minimizing the diet to as few ingredients as possible for a few weeks. If the offending food is eliminated, chances are that your dog will show great improvement.

Typically, these sorts of reactions come along after the dog has been eating a great variety of foods. In this case, discovering the food culprit can take time. Remember that your dog may continue to show a reaction for several weeks despite the fact that you have eliminated the allergen. Time and patience are required if you are serious about discovering what the problem might be.

Eating Grass

Many dogs enjoy eating new grass in the spring. The reason is unknown as this does not seem to have anything to do with an upset digestive tract. Other dogs eat grass and vomit afterwards. This suggests an upset digestive tract and many people believe that dogs use grass for a medicinal purpose. The problem with this behavior is that if the grass has been sprayed with chemicals, it can become a dangerous thing to ingest.

I find that grass eating can be stopped or minimized by looking at the diet carefully. If the foods are high in fat content, this alone can upset some dogs. Sometimes, a simple addition of alfalfa powder can be helpful in curbing this behavior. Some dogs seem to require a probiotic for at least a few days. Usually though, there is something in the diet itself that disagrees with the animal. Fiber content may need to be adjusted. I've had good success with the addition of a small amount of parsley to the diet. Adding more vegetables in general can be helpful as well, however, I see more success when veggie additions include greens.

Vomiting and Diarrhea

I will remind you that these things can be suggestive of a multitude of problems and your veterinarian should be consulted if your dog continues to vomit or have bad stool for more than a day or two. It also depends on how severe these symptoms are. One or two sloppy stools are not usually a problem. However, a dog that is vomiting and has many poor stools can dehydrate quickly, and should not be ignored.

If these reactions are not due to a more serious illness, look at the diet. Again, too much fat is a common problem. Some dogs can handle the same amount of fat for a long period of time only to suddenly become unable to digest the food that seemed to agree with them weeks earlier. If the diet is not full of fat, any ingredient can be a problem. Do not ignore supplements when you look at the diet. To too much of any ingredient can cause a reaction. Consider the possibility of a food allergen or other form of intolerance to a food. An allergic reaction can occur at any time despite the fact that your dog might have been thriving on a food for a long period of time.

Itchy Dogs

This is usually an allergic reaction. Once again, food may not be the problem as this could just as easily be a reaction to something in the environment. Have you changed your brand of detergent, fabric softener, floor cleaner, air freshener or other household cleanser? Have you installed new flooring of any sort? Is there new furniture in the house? Have you added a new supplement to the diet? Did you look really hard for fleas? These only touch on a huge number of possibilities. There are also seasonal allergies to consider - leaf mold, dust, dry indoor heat during cold months and of course, food. Since there is usually little we can do about environmental allergies and there are so many possibilities, diet may be the easiest place to start. An elimination diet is the way to discover if something in the diet is causing the problem.

Eating Dirt

There are living organisms in soil. It is not unnatural for a dog to eat soil but most people discourage the behavior. Once again, we need to consider the chemicals that may be found in sprayed gardens and the fact that these can leach into the soil.

I find that using the following items in this order can be helpful. Each item is used for one week before introducing the next one.

1.Probiotic
2.Multi B vitamin (always given *with* food to avoid stomach upset)
3.Alfalfa
4.Kelp or pinch of iodized table salt

Eating Feces

Also considered normal behavior in dogs, this is probably the one thing that drives us all a little crazy. Not only do we find it less than appealing to be kissed by a poop eater but feces can contain any number of things that we don't like - worm eggs, worms, infectious organisms and the like.

This habit is hard to break and many veterinarians believe it is usually a behavioral problem. Others see it as a nutritional deficiency of some kind. I believe it can be both.

Dogs seem to have an incredible sense of what their bodies need. True enough, most are just as apt to eat a big chunk of chocolate that

Dogs seem to have an incredible sense of what their bodies need. True enough, most are just as apt to eat a big chunk of chocolate that is toxic to them as they are to eat their meals. However, many dogs have taught me about their innate wisdom. Take Coco, a Standard Poodle living in Germany who developed a passion for raiding the herb garden. Her chosen herb was thyme, which happens to be effective against infections of the mouth. Coco had a history of these infections but managed to clear them up naturally much of the time.

I've known of too many examples of these behaviors to ignore them so when a dog eats feces, it may be a good idea to consider what feces might contain. If this is herbivore poop (dogs can't seem to resist horse and/or rabbit poop), your dog is getting some undigested fiber from plant matter. Try increasing the amount of greens in the diet to see if this is helpful. There is also some fat and bacteria in the stool. I usually suggest the following plan in an attempt to stop the behavior. Note that each step is given about a week before moving on to the next one.

1. Probiotic
2. Increase green vegetables
3. Digestive enzymes
4. Small increase of fat if the dog tolerates this
5. Multi B vitamin (always given *with* food to avoid stomach upset)
6. Small addition of well cooked grain

If the behavior stops during the dietary changes noted above, I see no reason to continue with all the suggestions. In other words, if your dog stops the behavior after he has been given a probiotic for one week, I would leave it at that.

If the dog finds cat feces irresistible, look at the diet and see if you are providing enough protein and fat. While an addition of either or both of these things can be helpful in curbing the behavior, I'm afraid that most dogs consider cat poop to be too much of a delicacy to pass up.

Sometimes, poop eating does not stop no matter what we do. In these cases, it may still be a dietary problem that we haven't discovered but I tend to believe that it is indeed a behavioral issue. Cleaning up after your dog has defecated is helpful. If the poop isn't lying around, he can't very well eat it.

He Seems Hyper

Most healthy dogs are bundles of energy. It is not uncommon for an owner to see this positive change, and be concerned that perhaps the dog has *too* much energy all of a sudden. In most cases, the dog is simply feeling great and wants to go, go, go! But there is another possibility.

Allergies can evoke almost any kind of response. One of them is hyperactivity. The dog that suddenly can't sit still may benefit from a diet change. As always, when considering allergies, an elimination diet is the best way to go. Before making any drastic changes, ask yourself if the behavior you see is *totally* unlike your dog or if it really does seem excessive. Obviously, some breeds are naturally more on the go than others.

Traveling

It is much easier to throw a bag of kibble in the trunk and go on a road trip with your dog, than it is to do the same when feeding a home-prepared diet. Many of my clients get stressed out over this idea but it doesn't have to be a problem if you think it through.

If you feed a cooked diet, baby foods such as chicken in broth, beef in broth etc, make it easy to provide the meat portion of the diet. Combine these with some rice from a take out restaurant and add a calcium source such as bone meal along with a multi vitamin. No, it is not a balanced meal but so what? It's not likely that you are going to be on the road for weeks on end.

If this suggestion doesn't appeal to you, consider the fact that almost any restaurant can provide you with some kind of meat right off the menu. Just ask to have it grilled without spices and most of your worries should disappear. Eggs are a good option as well. Should your dog do best on oatmeal, you can always buy the packets of instant oats. Simply order hot water from a restaurant, soak the oats and you're done.

Another option is to take a cooler, pack it with ice and food or just the vegetable portion of the diet (in small freezer bags). Add ice to the cooler as you go about your travels and these foods can remain fresh for a few days. If you are feeding a raw diet, there are many grocery stores to be found during your travels. A package of meat, marrow bones, beef oxtails and the veggies from your cooler should help you out.

Canned sardines are easy to take along and are easily combined with any number of foods to make a quick meal for your dog. They also eliminate the need to worry about adding Omega 3 to the diet for a while.

Remember that it is what you do most of the time that matters. A few days without the 'perfect' diet is not something to worry about. That is, unless like myself, you are living with a very sensitive dog that tolerates no dietary changes.

Even traveling with Zoey has not been a problem. I combine her meals in small plastic, freezer bags and always ensure that the hotel will allow me to use their freezer for storage. In the worst-case scenario, I've put her bags of food in the bar fridge in the room. It still keeps for 3-4 days.

Restaurant Take-Out and Convenience Store Foods-Quick Solutions

Eggs-cooked	Restaurant
Eggs-raw	Convenience/grocery store
Oatmeal	Restaurant
Yogurt	Convenience/grocery store
Canned fish	Convenience/grocery store
Baby foods-meats and vegetables	Convenience/grocery store
Stir fried meats	Restaurant
Canned beef stew	Convenience/grocery store
Raw meats/bones	Convenience/grocery store
Baby carrots for treats	Convenience/grocery store
Soup of the Day	Restaurant
Fruits	Convenience/grocery store
Cooked rice	Restaurant
Salad greens	Restaurant
Cottage or Ricotta cheese	Convenience/grocery store
Hamburger/chickenburger-plain	Restaurant
Frozen vegetables	Convenience/grocery store

Don't underestimate the power of a small kettle in your baggage. Frozen vegetables are already cooked. By pouring some boiling water over them, you have a quick addition to any meat source. The same is true for instant oatmeal.

Chapter 16
BLOOD VALUES

Before starting any new diet regime, I would strongly advise you to ask your veterinarian to do a full blood panel on your dog. By having this baseline to work from, both you and your vet are better equipped to note changes and discuss their significance. Some of my clients came to me because their dogs had blood work done and the values were out of the normal range. When I ask what the values were previously, many don't have a clue. So in fact, this same dog may have had a problem years ago or it may be something new. We can never know if we never checked prior to feeding in a new way.

There is another possibility. Perhaps the normal range of blood values that we currently use is not correct for dogs on a home-prepared diet. After all, they were based on dogs eating processed foods. I have no doubt that we will know more about this in the future, as veterinarians and other scientists explore possibilities. In my experience, dogs that eat a diet, which includes grains or a fair amount of vegetables, do not seem nearly as likely to have blood test results that fall outside of the normal range as those on a high meat diet.

My own dogs have blood values that fall within today's standards of normal ranges. Since they eat both cooked and raw foods, I can only guess that it is the composition of the diet that makes some difference.

The following is a quick overview of what some common blood values refer to. Please note that there may be other reasons for increased or decreased blood values and your veterinarian is your best guide.

Albumin

This is a blood protein. It affects the osmotic pressure (pressure of the fluid in cells) and transports fatty acids.

Increased levels point to dehydration.
Decreased levels may indicate a liver problem or loss through the gastrointestinal tract or kidneys.

Alk. Phos.

This is the lab short form for alkaline phosphatase, which is an enzyme. It is highly concentrated in the bones and liver.

Increased levels are considered normal in growing large breed puppies and may point to liver disease in adult dogs.
Decreased levels are not something that most veterinarians are concerned about.

ALT (SGPT)

This is the short form for alanine aminotransferase – an enzyme found in liver cells.

Increased levels are indicative of a variety of liver problems.

Amylase

This pancreatic enzyme works to help convert starch into sugar.

Increased levels may point to pancreatic disease, kidney or disease.
Decreased levels are not something that most veterinarians are concerned about.

AST (SGOT)

This is the short form for asparatate aminotransferase. It is an enzyme.

Increased levels may indicate tissue damage, liver or heart problems or inflammation of muscle.

Decreased levels are not something that most veterinarians worry about.

Bilirubin

Some tests will show both the direct and total bilirubin. The direct form is in fact a changed version. Hemoglobin is broken down and sent to the liver for chemical changes. It is then secreted into bile. The bile is delivered to the small intestine where it is converted into a waste product. This changed form is called direct bilirubin.

An increase in total bilirubin may point to liver disease, obstruction of the bile duct or destruction of red blood cells.

An increase of direct bilirubin may point to bile duct obstruction or liver disease.

A decrease of either direct or total bilirubin is not something most veterinarians worry about.

Calcium

This the circulating calcium level, not to be confused with the amount of calcium that the body is storing. Calcium is absorbed and released as the body requires it.

Increased levels may indicate an excess of vitamin D or protein in the system. It may also point to certain forms of cancer.

Decreased levels may indicate an under-active parathyroid gland or a problem with the pancreas.

Chloride

This shows the water balance of the body and the acid base.

Increased levels point to dehydration. As a result, the body may have become too acidic.

Decreased levels usually show up when there has been illness including vomiting, because there is a loss of gastric juices.

Cholesterol

This is a product that is produced by the liver and excreted in bile. Most dogs do not have a cholesterol problem like humans do.

Increased levels may point to obstruction of the bile duct or diabetes.

Decreased levels may be noted in a dog with diseases of the liver or kidneys.

CPK

This is an enzyme found in muscles including the heart.

Increased levels may be due to muscle damage. In some cases it may point to heart muscle damage. However a dog that has exerted himself or is overly excited may also show an increased level. It can also indicate damage to tissues during the blood collection procedure.

Decreased levels do not concern most veterinarians.

Creatinine

This is nitrogen waste product and specific to kidney function.

Increased levels may point to a kidney problem.

Decreased levels do not concern most veterinarians.

Glucose

Concentration of blood glucose levels can be influenced by how well the pancreas responds to variations in blood glucose by producing insulin.

Increased levels may be due to the animal having just been fed, stress, diabetes or over active adrenal glands.
Decreased levels may be due to starvation, tumors, too much insulin or improper functioning of the liver.

Lipase

This is a pancreatic enzyme that changes fatty acids.

Increased levels may point to pancreatitis or kidney problems.
Decreased levels are not a concern for most veterinarians.

Phosphorus

Blood levels can be affected by diet, kidney function and carbohydrate metabolism.

Increased levels may indicate kidney failure or a problem with the parathyroid gland.
Decreased levels may be due to diet (malnutrition) or malabsorption but can also be indicative of an overactive parathyroid gland.

Potassium

This is affected by aldosterone (a steroid) from the adrenal glands and is excreted by the kidneys.

Increased levels may be caused by under-active adrenal glands, kidney disease or a blockage of the urethra.
Decreased levels may be due to over active adrenal glands, diarrhea, vomiting or the increase of alkaline pH level in he blood.

Sodium

The amount of sodium is controlled by the aldosterone (a steroid) production of the adrenal glands.

Increased levels may be due to dehydration.
Decreased levels may be due to kidney disease, insufficient sodium in food, vomiting, diarrhea or an under-active adrenal gland.

Total Protein

A variety of proteins are produced by the liver and other organs.

Increased levels may point to tumors, chronic infection or dehydration.
Decreased levels may be due to starvation, kidney or liver disease.

Triglycerides

This shows the level of fat in the blood.

Increased levels can be due to an under-active thyroid, diabetes or pancreatitis.
Decreased levels do not concern most veterinarians

Urea (BUN)

An end product from the breakdown of protein, urea is found in urine and blood. A low protein diet translates into less urea being excreted through urine.

Increased blood levels may indicate kidney disease or other insult to the kidneys or dehydration.
Decreased levels may indicate a liver problem or a low protein diet.

Comparing Dogs to Wolves

When a dog has blood values that fall outside the normal range, some people wonder if perhaps these numbers would correlate to wolf blood values. This is especially the case when the dog had been eating a raw diet. After all, if our current range of values has been determined by looking at dogs eating processed diets, maybe the wolf values are a better indicator.

There are many factors that can affect blood values - from exertion to disease, a recent meal, diet in general, stress and many others circumstances. Attempting to compare apples to apples can be difficult even when we look at the same species.

Various labs use different equipment to analyze results and so, have different ranges of normal values. The challenge to find one lab that did the analysis for both wolves and dogs with the same equipment and using the same methods became my focus. I also wondered if we should·be comparing wild or captive wolves to our pets. After all, if we believe that that our dogs are wolves, they are captive wolves at best. The challenge in this instance was to find data on captive wolves that were being fed a raw diet.

The following information is presented for your interest.[13] You are looking at the blood value ranges of eleven free ranging wolves and twenty captive wolves that were in captivity for a minimum of two years while eating a raw, natural prey diet. These values come from the same lab using the same method of testing. The values for domestic dogs are not a part of this study. The value ranges for dogs are from the University of Illinois, which is the lab that produced the

---

[13] Serum Biochemistry Of Captive And Free-Ranging Gray Wolves (Canis Lupus) Constable et al (1998)

values for the wolves in the study, and have been provided by Dr. Constable.[14]

Factor	Captive	Free-Ranging	Dogs
Sodium (mEqL)	143.2 - 157.6	143.3 - 151.3	141 - 161
Potassium (mEqL)	3.6 - 5.2	4.3 - 5.5	3.9 - 5.7
Chloride (mEqL)	111.4 - 125.8	106.4 - 115.6	104 - 125
Calcium (mg/dl)	8.5 - 10.5	8 - 10.8	7.9 - 11.5
Phosphorus (mg/dl)	2 - 3.6	1 - 6.2	2.4- 6.5
Glucose (mg/dl)	85 - 137	N/A	65 - 127
Creatinine (mg/dl)	0.88 - 1.6	0.81 - 1.21	0.5 - 1.6
BUN (mg/dl)	4.4 - 34.8	N/A	7.0 - 31
Cholesterol (mg/dl)	107 - 231	102 - 234	109 - 315
ALT (U/L)	N/A	9- 209	17 - 87
Total Protein (g/dl)	5.55 - 6.43	5.13 – 6.85	5.4 -8.0
Albumin (g/dl)	3.45 - 4.29	3.34 - 4.66	2.1 - 4.3

---

[14] Peter D. Constable BVSc, MS, PhD, Diplomate ACVIM
Associate Professor & Section Head, Food Animal Medicine & Surgery
Department of Veterinary Clinical Medicine
College of Veterinary Medicine
University of Illinois

Chapter 17
DETECTIVE WORK

The following are some cases that I've worked with. By reading through a few of these stories, I hope that you begin to understand the various ways that dogs can show their nutritional distress and how some detective work can go a long way.

Sasha

Debbie asked me to come up with a diet plan for her eight year old German Shepherd Dog. They live in Australia where the weather can be quite hot during their summer months. Sasha seemed to have a problem with appetite. Basically, she just didn't seem to have one. Her energy level was quite high and she seemed happy but Debbie knew that at sixty two pounds, this dog was grossly underweight. Sasha had weighed seventy three pounds until she was switched to a home-prepared diet. Debbie was tempted to return to a diet of canned food but she wanted one last try at real food before giving up. At this point Sasha was eating 3 chicken necks and a total of 2 cups of muscle meats and vegetables, combined.

I asked Debbie if Sasha seemed to be hungrier at certain times of year. The reply was as expected. Yes, the dog did have a better appetite during the winter months.

Looking at Sasha's diet, I could find very little wrong with the composition. She ate a combination of raw and cooked foods and it seemed that if she would only eat what was given to her, things would be well. But Sasha is an individual and needs to be respected as such.

German Shepherds haven't been domesticated for very long. They are one of my favorite breeds to work with because they can present quite a challenge. In this case, I looked to the wolf in the wild for guidance. Not so much as composition of foods go because as I've mentioned, Sasha's diet as a whole seemed good. But wolves eat in cycles. As pups, they are the apple of the pack's eye and are fed whatever they desire. However, when they become teenagers, the same pack begins to see them as competition. The young wolves eat what is left over rather than have much of a choice. According to the personnel at wolf parks and the biologists I've spoken to, adult wolves have food preferences that tend to seasonal. In the fall, they tend to eat more of the organ meats and intestines of prey while sometimes leaving muscle meat behind. This works well for the teenagers of the pack because they need muscle meats at this stage of their lives. Nature seems to balance things out even to the degree of taste preference in the pack. By the time winter arrives, the adult wolves seem to choose the fattier portions of the prey carcass. This also makes sense since it is during the colder weather that more fat is required by the body.

Using the wolf preference as my guide, I suggested that Sasha be fed in much the same way. Rather than feeding a rotation of foods during one week or one month as Debbie had been doing, I suggested that during the summer months we feed her *very* lean meat combined with liver and vegetables. We excluded raw meaty bones for now and provided calcium though the use of eggshells. Sasha seemed to appreciate the change and ate well but would this continue? Indeed it did! She ate hungrily every night and it wasn't long before autumn arrived. The diet changed to include raw meaty bones and we stopped using eggshells. The liver was no longer used although we did manage to sneak in a bit of beef heart. When the diet was complete, it included far more fat than what was being used in the summer months. Sasha ate.

In the winter, the diet changed to more raw meaty bones, less meat and Sasha did not approve. This was the season that she was expected to eat more yet she seemed to be on strike. Even after Debbie put her on a two day fast, Sasha was walking away from any food offered. I have to admit that I wrestled with this problem for a couple of almost sleepless nights. Finally, I began to wonder if Sasha could benefit from some extra carbohydrates. This took me a long way away from my wolf role model but something urged me to try it. Combining Sasha's meat ration with one tablespoon of cooked oatmeal did the trick. She dove into her food and continued to do that right through the winter. We eliminated the oatmeal in the spring when she began to eat more muscle meats and quite a bit of vegetable matter.

I still hear from Debbie now and then. Sasha is three years older and still eating well throughout all four seasons. She weighs seventy- two pounds.

Pogo

Pogo is a walking miracle. Born in a puppy mill and rescued at the age of four, he came to Joanne in England with missing teeth, a coat that looked to be moth eaten, breath that could have sunk a ship, worms, colitis and if that's not enough, a pancreatitis attack after eating some raw lamb. He was almost unrecognizable as a Shih Tzu and seemed to be depressed most of the time.

As discussed in a previous chapter, I prefer to work with cooked meats when a dog is dealing with several health challenges at a time. Pogo was placed on a diet of lightly poached skinless, boneless chicken breast and mashed yams. He seemed to enjoy his meals and Joanne would run back and forth from work during her lunch break so that she could feed Pogo three times per day. This schedule allowed Pogo to eat small meals that his digestive tract could tolerate. It took about a month before this little dog seemed to feel better and acted happier. At that point, we began to introduce supplements and a rotation of proteins.

Joanne called me one day and there was excitement in her voice. Was it possible that diet could make this drastic a change, she asked? Pogo hadn't had a bath in a month yet his skin had no odor. His coat seemed to be growing in nicely. I was pleased of course, but I couldn't resist reminding Joanne that she hadn't given me any news about Pogo's stool. After all, colitis is a concern at times as I know from my own dog. In a lovely English accent, Joanne said " His stool is jolly good and has been for several weeks now".

I am delighted to report that in the last picture I received, Pogo looked incredible. His long coat was glistening. The note that Joanne sent me said that this little guy was thriving on a multitude of foods, which she is more than happy to prepare for him.

Annie

Greg brought his Rottweiler-Labrador cross home from the shelter when she was less than one year old. Annie stole his heart right away. She was his girl through and through. Despite her size (ninety five pounds), Annie thought she was a baby and would cuddle up with Greg on the sofa while he clutched on to a few inches of a cushion in an attempt to lie down and watch television.

The love that Greg showered on Annie was highly rewarded when he collapsed on the driveway one day. Annie threw herself through a window to reach him and chased down a neighbor on the street to get their attention. This person called 911 and Greg pulled through his heart attack. Neither Greg nor I are sure if this would have been the case had Annie not reacted the way she did.

Amazingly, Annie only needed a few stitches to sew up the damage that her feat of courage had created. Greg wanted a diet that might help Annie heal faster and keep her healthy for the next one hundred years. Can't say that I blame him. This is an extraordinary girl!

Annie loves beef and does well on it. Her diet consists mainly of beef muscle meat combined with beef heart and liver, an assortment of vegetables and small amounts of cooked grain when she pleads for some of Greg's rice. Greg suffers from several immune system problems so he didn't want a raw diet anywhere near him. He opted for a cooked diet that included bone meal as a source of calcium. Annie also enjoys chicken, lamb and any kind of fish she can get. I've never known a dog to be quite *that* enthralled with fish!

It hasn't been one hundred years but Greg thinks Annie will be around for a long time.

Lassie

Yes, there really is a Lassie and she happens to be a three year old Collie living in Germany. Hilda's children named the dog. Lassie is one of three dogs in the family and she always ate what the others did; a home-prepared, raw diet. While the other dogs seemed to be doing well, Lassie suffered from itchy skin and a poor coat. Hilda judiciously added good oils to the food but nothing seemed to help and by the time she contacted me, Lassie was chewing herself raw.

The diet was full of what *should* have been wonderful foods but Lassie obviously disagreed. We tried an elimination diet and that seemed to help a little bit but not nearly enough. I decided that there had to be some other clue and asked Hilda about supplements. As it turned out, there was not much consistency. Whatever happened to be on sale is what Lassie received that week or month. While the dog was receiving the same *types* of supplements, the brands changed routinely.

Knowing that there can be vast differences in quality, I asked Hilda to tell me about the lab analyses on the supplements. She didn't know and neither did the personnel at the store. We decided to use the Swiss Herbal brand since I'm very sure of the quality. Lo and behold, Lassie began to mutilate herself less and less until she stopped doing it altogether! Her skin looked great and her beautiful coat came back for everyone to admire.

The lesson that Lassie would suggest you take home with you is that sometimes the food isn't the problem. Look at your supplements and find out what's in them. To this day, Lassie gets a soy free version of Vitamin E. If the Vitamin E you use is derived from soy (and most are today), it can be the reason that your dog seems to scratch more often than you'd like. Look at the entire ingredient list on supplement labels. Herbs that are added as a 'bonus' may seem good to *you* but they can nevertheless trigger a reaction in your dog. Color additives can be a problem as well. Try to find the purest sources of supplements and stick with them even if they're not the least expensive on the market.

Loli

Also know as Lollipop, this little Papillion is a classic case of a dog trying to tell us something! Loli was a well-behaved girl until the herb garden in the yard began to sprout. The new dill was irresistible to her and she managed to eat huge amounts of it before she could be stopped.

When I consult with a client, I ask a lot of questions that some people think are a little odd. For instance, I ask if the dog hides after eating or if there is any other behavior that seems not quite right. I find that dog people usually have a sixth sense about these things. In Loli's case, Jenny (the human counter-part in this story) had noticed that yes, the dog always hid after eating but she hadn't really given this much thought.

Detective work means that you have to take pieces of a puzzle and try to put them together. While hiding after eating is not the norm, some dogs simply do this as a way of taking their quiet time away from the noise of the family. But Loli lives alone with Jenny. There are no other animals or people around and it seemed unlikely that this hiding behavior was just down time for the dog. More likely, Loli had some discomfort and was doing what most dogs do in this situation. They prefer to be alone. They hide.

Amongst its other properties, dill helps soothe the stomach. Putting these two pieces together was easy. Loli was probably in distress after eating (hiding was her way of telling us so) and she loved dill because it soothed her stomach.

At this point we changed Loli's diet. Whereas she'd been eating a variety of foods, she was now restricted to turkey and rice. This seemed to agree with her and as time went on, we were able to add supplements and a few vegetables. Loli cannot tolerate much in the way of greens but does well on root veggies such as turnip and carrots. She stopped hiding after eating her meals and wanted to play instead. To the best of my knowledge, Loli is still doing well today and her passion for dill is a thing of the past.

Jangles

Don held on to the leash and Jangles tried to move toward me. This was the first time I met Jangles and it was all I could do to maintain my composure. This Rhodesian Ridgeback could barely walk and the sadness in his eyes was pitiful. Jangles had canine lymphoma.

Diet is not a cure for cancer and I never pretend that it can work miracles, but it can go a long way in helping the animal gain strength. The problem is that chemotherapy can make the dog feel quite awful and nauseous, so getting that dog to eat is a challenge. To top it all off, Jangles had sores and ulcers in his mouth.

I am not fond of raw diets for a dog that is in this bad a shape. In my opinion, open sores and a weakened immune system call for a cooked diet. Jangles first home cooked meal consisted of boiled chicken, shredded in a food processor, with the addition of boiled squash. Broth was added to this in order to make the food watery and allow Jangles to lap at it, rather than expect him to chew. At first, he couldn't manage even this. The poor guy would slurp his food only to have it dribble out of his mouth. Don was frantic. I wasn't doing much better but had to keep a stiff upper lip. Jangles rewarded both of us by managing to lap up about a cup of food the next day.

Don and I celebrated good news almost daily. Jangles really seemed to enjoy his food even though much of it ended up on the floor rather than in his mouth. It took only two weeks before Jangles was eating well. No more food all over the kitchen floor. Every drop was staying in his mouth and his sloppy stool was now firm.

We began to add supplements including a tablespoon of flaxseed oil daily, a multi B vitamin as well as vitamins C and E. A multi vitamin/mineral was also included. The diet changed at this point as well. Jangles ate a *lot* of green vegetables. From broccoli to kale, spinach, lettuce, watercress, celery and parsley, he loved them all. He was lucky to be able to tolerate these, as not all dogs can handle such large amounts of greens in the diet. We wanted antioxidants and green veggies seemed appropriate in this case. A few weeks later, we introduced eggs, turkey, fish and rabbit. By now Jangles was putting on weight, acting happy and eating well.

Despite the fact that I don't believe that diet alone was what saved Jangles, he lived another three, happy years. Maybe diet helped him during this time. I certainly hope so and believe it did. Don called me to say that one morning he woke up but Jangles didn't. There had been no indication of illness and no pain that Don was aware of. Jangles was thirteen years old.

Pickles

Yes, I know. I had the same reaction when I first heard what this dog was named. But you'd have to meet her to understand. Pickles is a mixed breed with the personality of, well, a pickle! Sweet and sour, tangy and fiery, she is definitely Miss Personality with a mind of her own.

Pickles was ten years old and if she hadn't always been a fuss-budget, she certainly was one now. Her humans, Kate and John, were at wit's end because Pickles refused to eat. The veterinarian advised them that their dog was healthy so obviously Pickles was just spoiled.

One of the questions I ask when I begin a consultation is what has the dog been eating? In this case, Pickles had been eating a variety of dry and canned diets, all in an attempt to get her interested in *something*. She would sniff the bowl and walk away. Only when she was desperately hungry would she bother to eat a few bites. The brand didn't seem to matter. She just wasn't going to eat this stuff despite the fact that she had lost four pounds. Given that her optimum weight was forty pounds, this translated to ten percent of her body weight - not a good thing!

We gave Pickles some lamb and rice and she ate it. We tried chicken and veggies. She ate that too. As a matter of fact, Pickles ate everything she was offered and never lifted her head out of the bowl. Her cast iron stomach didn't have a problem with any food and she could easily handle both cooked and raw diets. This made life easy for Kate who was the dog chef in the household. On a hectic day, she could crack a couple of eggs, use some frozen vegetables or leftover grain, add a multi vitamin/mineral tablet and some oil and Pickles would eat with gusto. She never stopped enjoying her meals but variety is key for this dog. Pickles enjoys at least four different meals weekly and has regained the weight she lost.

I think that Kate spoke for Pickles when she called to tell me that the dog had probably had enough of processed foods and was demanding home-prepared meals in her old age. After all, a lifetime of canned and bagged foods must get pretty tiresome!

Mercedes

Alison decided that if she couldn't afford the car, she could at least give her dog this recognizable name. Mercedes was an eleven-year-old Labrador Retriever with a history of inflammatory bowel disease and arthritis. She had spent many years taking prednisone, which caused her to drink excessively and urinate at all hours of the day and night.

Alison had developed some health problems herself over the last few years, and was beginning to look into alternative therapies for this reason. One of the first things she did was change her own diet and it seemed only right that Mercedes could benefit from this as well.

Mercedes had been placed on numerous diets throughout her life so she had been exposed to a variety of proteins. Alison was concerned that we would not be able to find a novel protein for her. In my experience, a dog may react to a canned or bagged food, yet be able to tolerate the same protein when it is in the form of real food. Perhaps the other ingredients in pet food were a problem for Mercedes because she certainly had no trouble with either chicken or turkey as her meat sources. She could eat eggs as well.

Alison was diligent in following her dog's lead. When Mercedes had sloppy stool every time she was fed green vegetables, it was obvious that greens would not be a part of the diet. When Mercedes had gas after eating lamb, we knew that this meat was not for her. Things became clear quickly, and as a result, two months later, we had a diet plan that Mercedes did well on. So well in fact, that she no longer required medication for the inflammatory bowel disease since she didn't have any more bouts of vomiting and diarrhea.

Oliver

Nobody really knows what breeds might be in Oliver's background. He definitely looks to be part Malamute but the rest is anyone's guess.

Oliver had several problem and they all began when he was 3 years old. At first it was an overgrowth of yeast in his ears. That was followed by inconsistent stool and finally Oliver developed an acid urine.

Linda was feeding an impressive assortment of raw foods to her boy, and did not believe that dogs had a requirement for carbohydrates. Since many northern breeds seem to do very well on a high meat and fat diet with little carbohydrates, Linda felt that Oliver should thrive on this as well.

A need for carbohydrates in the canine diet has never been established and I liked the fact that Linda had done some research and knew about this. Then again, I haven't found any impressive studies to show that carbohydrates are problematic either. But Oliver had acid urine, so proof or no proof, we just wanted him to feel better and stop licking private areas that were now red, from irritation. We reduced the amount of meat in the diet and added more vegetables. This boy was now eating 40% Kcal from protein instead of the 60% that he had been fed in the past. The difference was made up in green leafy vegetables. Oliver developed sloppy stool almost instantly. After some juggling, we discovered that by including brown rice as 20% of the total diet, Oliver not only maintained great stool quality, but his urine pH rose to 6.5 - in other words, it was perfect! Oliver did very well with grain.

With his urine pH under control and his stool being cause for celebration at Linda's household, it was time to work on the gunky ears. My first step is to introduce a probiotic so we started off with that. It took two attempts with different brands to find the right thing but a few weeks later, Oliver had nice clean ears. There seemed to be no reason to add anything else to the diet as Oliver was now feeling wonderful.

Ordinarily, when I see a dog with yeast troubles and inconsistent stool, I think about food allergies and a depressed immune system. If not for the acid urine, which demanded to be addressed first, I might have tried to find a food culprit, rather than looking at this as a fiber or carbohydrate issue. Oliver taught me that sometimes what we think is more than one problem, can nevertheless be rectified with only one step. His acid urine and sloppy stool were resolved with an increase in carbohydrates. Oliver is one of the dogs that made me put the books down and really look at him and learn. Thanks, Oliver!

Chapter 18
THE LAST WORD

Your dog has invaluable information to share with you. He or she has the ability to lead you in directions that you may never have considered. Dogs are intelligent animals that can understand our body language despite the fact that it is totally different from their own. They can understand several words and commands in our languages. Can we understand even one word of theirs?

I've tried to imagine what it would be like to leave everything I know and find myself in another world where everyone is a stranger. If I couldn't understand their language but was sometimes reprimanded for displeasing these strangers, I'm not sure that I would be very trusting, much less loving. Our dogs find themselves in this situation and provide nothing but love and caring even when we don't deserve it. They are inspirational animals and dog lovers know it! If only we could bridge the communication gap, we might be able to learn so much more.

There is an old saying - lack of proof doesn't mean lack of efficacy. We may not always be able to prove things scientifically but there is no doubt that dogs try to communicate with us in their way. Simply because we don't understand their language doesn't mean that they deserve less respect for their needs.

Your dog is a unique individual with every right to live a long and healthy life. He may not be able to do it if we ignore what he tries to tell us and stick to previously formed opinions about what the perfect diet might be. We are not wise enough to know this. Only your dog knows it. By all means, the last word belongs to him or her!

Cooking Measure Equivalents

1 Tablespoon	3 teaspoons
1/16 cup	1 Tablespoon
1/8 cup	2 Tablespoons
1/6 cup	2 Tablespoons + 2 teaspoons
1/4 cup	4 Tablespoons
1/3 cup	5 Tablespoons + 1 teaspoon
3/8 cup	6 Tablespoons
1/2 cup	8 Tablespoons
3/4 cup	12 Tablespoons
1 cup	48 Tablespoons

Metric Conversion

Multiply	By	To Get
Fluid Ounces	29.57	grams
Ounces (dry)	28.35	grams
Grams	0.0353	ounces
Grams	0.0022	pounds
Kilograms	2.21	pounds
Pounds	453.6	grams
Pounds	0.4536	kilograms
Quarts	0.946	liters
Liters	1.0567	quarts

Resources

All You Ever Wanted To Know About Herbs For Pets
Gregory Tilford and Mary Wulff-Tilford
Bowtie Press, 1999
Stunning! A comprehensive look at the use of herbs, including interactions and contraindications.

Dr. Pitcairn's Complete Guide to Natural Heath for Dogs and Cats
Richard Pitcairn, DVM, PhD and Susan Hubble Pitcairn
Rodale Press, 1995
Natural rearing of cats and dogs including discussion of diets and sample recipes.

Four Paws, Five Directions
Cheryl Schwartz, DVM
Celestial Arts Publishing, 1996
Chinese Veterinary Medicine, including the principles behind the foods chosen to address medical conditions.

Complementary and Alternative Veterinary Medicine: Principles and Practices
Allan Schoen, Susan Wynn
Mosby, 1998
Written by veterinarians for other vet professionals, this book discusses every modality imaginable. Nutrient requirements are discussed at length.

The Complete Herbal Handbook for the Dog and Cat
Juliette de Bairacli Levy
Faber & Faber 1995
Stresses no vaccines, raw diets and herbal remedies.

Fats That Heal, Fats That Kill: The Complete Guide to Fats and Oils, Cholesterol and Human Health
Udo Erasmus

Rev&Updtd edition, December 1993
Detailed discussion about the roles of fats and their properties.

Food Pets Die For
Ann Martin
NewSage Press 1997
An investigation into the pet food industry by a woman who is not faint of heart. This book speaks truths that have only recently been publicized in newspapers.

Protect Your Pet: More Shocking Facts
Ann Martin
NewSage Press 2001
Discusses the dangers of commercial pet foods, excessive vaccinations, and the reasons that the author will not feed raw meat diets to her own pets.

The Wolf : The Ecology and Behavior of an Endangered Species
L. David Mech
University of Minnesota Press , eighth printing, 1995
The ecology and behavior of wolves are discussed in fascinating detail.

Keep Your Dog Healthy the Natural Way
Pat Lazarus
The Ballantine Publishing Group 1999
Holistic veterinarians offer thoughts and advice on the natural care of pets.

Canine Nutrition
William D. Cusick
Doral Publishing Inc. 1997
The author believes that every breed requires a diet, based on the country where it originated.

Natural Nutrition for Dogs and Cats: The Ultimate Diet
Kymythy Schultze
Hay House Inc. 1998
Feeding of raw foods and bones, based on the prey role model.

Enzymes: A Practical Introduction to Structure, Mechanism and Data Analysis
Robert Allen Copelan
Vch Pub 1996
Detailed presentation of chemical bonds and reactions, chemical mechanisms, structural components and more.

Give Your Dog A Bone
Ian Billinghurst B.V Sc, B.Sc Dip. Ed.
Ian Billinghurst, 1993
Promotes bones and raw foods as the only viable option to keeping a dog healthy

Home-prepared Dog and Cat Diets: The Healthful Alternative
Donald R. Strombeck, DVM. PhD
Iowa State University Press, 1999
In depth discussion including cooked diets for various conditions and diseases.

Natural Dog Care : A Complete Guide To Holistic Health Care for Dogs
Celeste Yarnall, PhD
Charles Tuttle Co 1998
A spiritual alternative with discussions that include, vaccinations, diet, and other material.

Holistic Guide For a Healthy Dog
Wendy Volhad and Kerry Brown, DVM
Howell Book House, 2000
Discussion includes diet, vaccines, kinesiology and more.

Raw Meaty Bones
Tom Lonsdale
Rivetco P/L, 2001

 Discusses challenges faced by the author within his veterinary community and pet food industry, as well as what he feels is the correct diet.

The Nature of Animal Healing
Martin Goldstein, DVM
The Ballantine Publishing Company, 1999
A holistic viewpoint that includes the theory behind the 'healing crisis', detoxification, and various therapies.

The Hidden Life of Dogs
Elizabeth Marshall Thomas
Houghton Mifflin Company, 1993
Observations and insight into the behavior of dogs left to their own devices while living with humans.

The Lost History of The Canine Race : Our 15,000-Year Love Affair with Dogs
Mary Elizabeth Thurston
Andrews and McMeel, 1996
The evolution of dogs as human companions, with a focus on cultural changes.

Love, Miracles and Animal Healing
Allan Schoen, DVM
Fireside, 1996
Heartwarming stories with a focus on the human animal bond - some diet ideas are included.

Kindred Spirits
Allen Schoen, DVM
Broadway Books, 2001
Stories and studies that show the impact that all species have on each other.

Pet Loss: A Spiritual Guide
Eleanor L. Harris
Llewellyn Publications, 1998

A gentle guide through the grieving process.

The Body Language and Emotion of Dogs
Myrna M Mileni, DVM
William Morrow and Company, 1986
A perspective that includes the scientific suggestion of dogs interacting with their owners only for the sake of survival.

How To Get Well: Dr. Airola's Handbook of Natural Healing
Airola, P. Phoenix AZ
Health Plus Publishers, 1984
Easy to understand discussions about healthy lifestyles.

Return to the Joy of Health: Natural Medicine and Alternative
Treatment for All Your Health Complaints
Rona, Zoltan P. and Martin, Jeanne Marie
Alive Books, 1995
Practical and comprehensive with a focus on nutrition.

Childhood Illness and The Allergy Connection
Rona, Zoltan P. Rocklin,
Prima Books, 1996
Making a connection between illness and allergies.

INDEX